knitting in the sun

32 PROJECTS FOR WARM WEATHER

knitting in the sun

32 PROJECTS FOR WARM WEATHER

BY KRISTI PORTER

Wiley Publishing, Inc.

Library of Congress Cataloging-in-Publication Data:
Porter, Kristi.
  Knitting in the sun : 32 projects for warm weather / by Kristi Porter.
    p. cm.
  Includes index.
  ISBN-13: 978-0-470-41666-2
  ISBN-10: 0-470-41666-1
  1. Knitting--Patterns. 2. Hot weather clothing. I. Title.
  TT825.P66 2009
  746.43'20432--dc22

                              2008054106

Printed in the United States of America

10 9 8 7 6 5 4 3

Book production by Wiley Publishing, Inc., Composition Services

credits

acquisitions editor
Roxane Cerda

project editor
Carol Pogoni

editorial manager
Christina Stambaugh

publisher
Cindy Kitchel

vice president and
executive publisher
Kathy Nebenhaus

interior design
Elizabeth Brooks

cover design
Wendy Mount

photography
Stephen Simpson

acknowledgments

It's been a pleasure to write this book because of the people involved in creating it. I feel that *Knitting in the Sun* is the work of many friends, some of whom I did not have the pleasure to know until this project began, and others whom I've known for a long time, but not in the roles they've played here. In many senses, this book is a product of my neighborhood, real and virtual, and to be able to say that is truly gratifying.

Without exception, everyone I called upon worked energetically and enthusiastically to do what I asked of them, whether it was knitting under tight deadlines, acting goofy in front of the camera, giving up days off, or catching my mistakes. It is my pleasure to thank them here:

The dedicated people at Wiley Publishing, especially Roxane Cerda and Carol Pogoni, whose counsel and guidance made the journey from nothing to something not only possible, but enjoyable.

The designers featured in this book, who not only inspired me with their designs, but with their professionalism and dedication to creating this collection.

Stephen Simpson, whose beautiful photography makes this book a joy to look at.

The models who bring these designs to life: Courtney Avvampato, Ella Bleicher, Zoe Bleicher, Sarah Englehardt, Laura Murphy, Zia Simpson, Sarah Temerlin, and Mia Vaughnes.

My family, whose patience and support allow me to do what I love.

The regulars at Knitting in La Jolla, who are always generous with their feedback and enthusiasm for the craft.

To all of you, my thanks and gratitude!

knitting in the sun

15

151

24

76

7

20

130

69

100

80

39

134

147

27

42

111

11

117

160

123

155

30

104

63

167

91

141

87

51

33

57

47

table of contents

introduction

Icelandic yoked pullovers. Classic Aran fishermen's sweaters. Warm, woolen mittens. These are the things that knitting dreams are made of. But lots of knitting patterns are simply out-of-bounds for people living in warmer climates. We love to look through all those books and magazines, but we have to ignore many patterns or to wonder and worry about what will happen if we substitute a cooler bamboo or cotton yarn for wool.

So, I wanted to create a collection of patterns that weren't simply summer clothes, but lovely items that you can wear throughout the year in warmer climates—and wear in the sunnier months, regardless of where you live. Truthfully, since most of us live and work in temperature-controlled environments, we all need knits that are comfortable to wear at 70 degrees.

I solicited designs from a variety of popular knitwear designers and challenged them to create pieces they would want to wear in their own favorite hot spots. Cover-ups suitable for days like we have in the desert Southwest, where the temperature can shift from 55 to 85 and back again in twelve hours. Or an ensemble that can take you from home, to work, out to the movies, and off for a stroll on the beach. The goal was to create garments that provide coverage and style without extra bulk or too much warmth, as well as accessories that are just right for summer weather. And I am so excited by what the designers came up with! This book contains over 30 interesting and ambitious designs that are flattering and promise plenty of knitting pleasure.

design decisions

A number of design elements make these knits ready for sunny days. Of course, lightweight yarns keep these projects from feeling too hot and heavy, but that doesn't mean you'll knit only on the smallest needles in your quiver. Looser gauges, the use of lace details, and open stitches that allow air to flow through are techniques the designers used to keep garments cooler and the knitting interesting.

Choosing the right materials to knit with is also important. The fibers used in this book's patterns compose a surprising and interesting list, including things you've probably tried before and lots you haven't. There are typical "summer" yarn choices like linen, silk, and cotton, and some smart and interesting animal/vegetable blends that bring together the best of both worlds like alpaca and soy, linen and mohair, silk and wool. Warmer fibers like mohair, wool, and alpaca aren't out of bounds as long as they are paired with design details that help them keep their cool. And appropriate, comfortable yarn choices mean you don't have to wear more than you want to beneath your knits.

Many of the pieces in this collection are well suited to layering. You can pair sleeveless and short-sleeved tops with a jacket or wrap when things get chilly. And just take off or put on a cardigan or cover-up when the temperature shifts. Inventive wraps and scarves will dress you up without weighing you down.

When you combine all these design decisions, the results are wonderful pieces that women can really wear in all seasons. There are projects that will appeal to a broad range of tastes, ages, and body types.

how to use this book

The patterns in this book are sized to fit women from extra small through plus sizes. All patterns follow the sizing conventions set by the Craft Yarn Council of America. (You can find details on these sizing standards at http://yarnstandards.com.) If you are a medium according to these guidelines, then the medium is the correct size for you to knit throughout the book. Finished measurements are provided for all patterns and the accompanying schematics provide more detail on the sizing if you want to alter a pattern for a custom fit.

The patterns in this book cover a range of difficulty. If you are a new knitter, you will certainly find patterns here that are within your grasp. And seasoned stitchers will find patterns to challenge them, too. Since what is new, or difficult, varies so much from knitter to knitter, I have offered information on the skills used in the pattern rather than a ranking system. Use this information combined with a quick read through the pattern to help you decide if it's the right pattern for you to knit. If a term or technique is unfamiliar to you, turn to the appendices for help with the abbreviations used throughout this book and for step-by-step instructions on special knitting techniques.

Please take a moment to learn more about the wonderful designers whose patterns are featured throughout this book. You will find brief biographies as well as contact information for the companies who provided yarns for these projects at the back of the book.

Many of the patterns in the book that feature lace or other stitch patterns rely on charts. Since knitters want to carry these charts with them while they knit and be able to make notes on the charts, you will be pleased to know that all the charts in the book are available as downloadable files at **www.wiley.com/go/knittinginthesun**.

Whether you are looking to expand your work wardrobe, create the perfect accessory for your summer vacation, or indulge in a bit of whimsy, I know that you will enjoy this knitting collection as much as I do. I hope this book will inspire you to knit—and wear the things that you create!—year round, whether you really are knitting in the sun, or just dreaming about it.

ACCESSORIES

WINDANSEA
sun hat

WINDANSEA

sun hat

by Kristi Porter

O n bright, sunny days, I'm underdressed without a sunhat. I hadn't thought to knit one until I started thinking of designs for this book. Inspired by Annie Modesitt's knitted millinery, I decided to give it a go. I've always loved the simple organic spirals created by regular decreases on the crowns of hats and decided to play them up on this lovely, light sunhat. This sunhat provides just enough cover to keep the sun off your face, but never feels hot or heavy.

pattern notes

This pattern uses millinery wire to support the broad brim. You can find it online and in some craft stores. You can also substitute any other sturdy, rustproof wire.

directions

CO 192 (200) sts on circular needle. Join to knit in the round, being careful not to twist sts.

brim

Set-up Round: *K24 (25), place marker (pm), rep from * around, using contrasting marker last to indicate the end of round.

Round 1: *K to 3 sts before marker, yo, sk2p, slip marker (sm), rep from * around.

Round 2: Knit.

Rep these 2 rounds until 80 (88) sts rem. There will be 10 (11) sts between each set of markers.

SIZE
S (L)

To fit 20–22 (22–24)" circumference heads

FINISHED MEASUREMENTS
Outside circumference, stretched: 42 (44)"

Inside circumference, unstretched: 16 (17½)"

MATERIALS
- Berroco *Seduce* (47% rayon, 25% linen, 17% silk, 11% nylon; 100 yd. per 40g skein); color: 4448 Verdigris; 2 (2) skeins
- US 6 (4mm) circular needle, 16" length (*or size needed to match gauge*)
- US 6 (4mm) double-pointed needles
- Size G (4mm) crochet hook
- 50" length of 18-gauge millinery wire, or other similar wire

continued ➤

➤ **continued**

- 1 package K1C2 Rainbow Elastic Thread (3mm Bulky; 25 yd. per package); color: 60
  (Use a color that matches or is slightly darker than your yarn.)
- 8 stitch markers, 1 contrasting
- Tapestry needle

GAUGE

20 sts × 28 rows = 4" in St st

SKILLS USED

double-pointed needles, knitting in the round, decreasing, yarn overs, single crochet

body of hat

Round 1: *K8 (9), yo, skp, sm, rep from * around.

Round 2 and all even rounds: Knit.

Round 3: *K7 (8), yo, skp, k to marker, sm, rep from * around.

Round 5: *K6 (7), yo, skp, k to marker, sm, rep from * around.

Round 7: *K5 (6), yo, skp, k to marker, sm, rep from * around.

Round 9: *K4 (5), yo, skp, k to marker, sm, rep from * around.

Round 11: *K3 (4), yo, skp, k to marker, sm, rep from * around.

Round 13: *K2 (3), yo, skp, k to marker, sm, rep from * around.

Round 15: *K1 (2), yo, skp, k to marker, sm, rep from * around.

Round 17: *K0 (1), yo, skp, k to marker, sm, rep from * around

For larger size only:

Round 19: *Yo, skp, k to marker, sm, rep from * around.

Both sizes continue:

Next round: Knit.

Next round: *K to 1 st before marker, sl next st to right needle, remove marker, sl st back to left needle, replace marker, yo, skp, rep from * around. (The marker should sit between the yarn over and the decrease.)

Next round: Knit.

Next round: *K to 2 sts before marker, yo, skp, sm, rep from * around.

Next round: Knit.

crown

Switch to dpns to shape crown.

Round 1: *K to 3 sts before marker, yo, sk2p, sm, rep from * around.

Round 2: Knit.

Rep these 2 rounds until 16 sts rem.

Next round: *K2tog, rep from * around.

finishing

Cut yarn, leaving a 6" tail. Use a tapestry needle to thread yarn through rem sts. Pull to close. Bring yarn through all sts again and weave in the end to secure it.

Cut millinery wire to approximately 50". Form a circle with the wire, overlap the two ends by about 5", and hold in place with clothespins or a piece of tape.

Using crochet hook and yarn, single crochet in each st around the hat brim (single crochet twice in each eyelet), capturing the wire in the crochet casing. To do so, attach the yarn to the hat, then *insert the crochet hook from RS into 1 st on the edge of the brim, bring the hook *under* the wire, wrap the yarn around the hook and pull through, bring the yarn *over* the wire, wrap the yarn around the hook and pull through both loops. Rep from * until you have concealed all but 2" of wire. Adjust the size of the wire circle so the brim lies flat. Trim the ends of the wire, if necessary, and securely tape the overlapped ends to secure. Continue crocheting to finish encasing the wire. Cut yarn end and pull through last loop to secure.

Weave in ends.

With a tapestry needle, on the WS of work, thread elastic through a row of sts at the base of the crown. Adjust to fit comfortably on the head. Run elastic through another row of sts, double-check the fit, and fasten off the ends of the elastic.

BARDINI
summer cloche

BARDINI
summer cloche

by Julia Trice

A fun hat is just right for a summer day. This cloche, knit in linen with a woven texture, fits the bill perfectly. If you've never tried a herringbone stitch pattern, then you'll be intrigued by the result, which is softly reminiscent of a straw hat. Wear Bardini with the brim rolled up, or adorn it with a flapper-style ribbon or pin.

pattern notes

Work your flat swatch "in the round" as follows: CO 28 sts on a circular needle, work Round 1 of the Miniature Herringbone Pattern, ending with k1 tbl. Do not join, but move the sts to the opposite end of the needle and do not turn, as you would to make I-cord. Strand the yarn very loosely across the back of the work and work the second "round," ending with k1. Continue in this manner until you complete the swatch. Wet and block the swatch before measuring your gauge.

In the Miniature Herringbone Pattern, you will work each stitch twice: once with the stitch before it and once with the stitch after it. Because you work each stitch with the stitches on either side of it, you need to remove the marker while you work the stitch before it and then replace it after you move that stitch to the right-hand needle.

miniature herringbone pattern

Round 1 and all odd rounds: *K2tog tbl, dropping only the first of the 2 sts off the LH needle, rep from * to end.

Round 2 and all even rounds: *K2tog, dropping only the first of the 2 sts off the LH needle, rep from * to end.

decreasing

Even-Round Dec: K3tog tbl, dropping the first 2 sts off the LH needle, but leaving the third st on the LH needle so you can work it with the following st.

SIZE
One size fits most adult women

FINISHED MEASUREMENTS
Brim circumference: 28½"

Hat circumference: 21¾"

MATERIALS
- Louet *Euroflax* Sport Weight (100% linen; 270 yd. per 100g skein); color: 5 Goldilocks; 1 skein
- US 7 (4.5mm) circular needle, 24" length *(or size needed to match gauge)*
- US 7 (4.5mm) circular needle, 16" length
- US 7 (4.5mm) double-pointed needles
- Tapestry needle
- 7 stitch markers, plus 1 contrasting marker

GAUGE
28 sts × 25 rows = 4" in Miniature Herringbone Pattern, blocked

SKILLS USED
knitting in the round, double-pointed needles, unusual stitch pattern, decreasing

Odd-Round Dec: K3tog, dropping the first 2 sts off the LH needle, but leaving the third st on the LH needle so you can work it with the following st.

directions

NOTE Due to the stitch pattern and the yarn, the first few rounds will require patience. Do not work too tightly. Use a finger to keep the second stitch in a pair on the left-hand needle while transferring the new stitch to the right-hand needle. After the first few rounds, the going will get substantially easier!

brim

With the 24" circular needle, use the cable cast-on to CO 200 sts loosely, placing markers every 25 sts. Place the contrasting marker to indicate the beg of round and join the work, being careful not to twist sts.

The cloche is worked in Miniature Herringbone Pattern throughout.

Round 1: Work in patt to last st of round, sl last st, remove marker, sl st back to the LH needle and work the st as the first st of the second round of the patt. Place marker (pm) on the RH needle after you complete the first st. You will work every round of the cloche this way, working the last st of each round as if it were the first st of the following round and then replacing the beg of round marker.

Rounds 2 and 3: Work in patt.

Round 4 (Dec Round): *Work in patt to 3 sts before marker, dec (use Even-Round Dec—see above), sl next st and marker to RH needle, remove marker, sl st back to LH needle, work next st of round, replace marker, rep from * to end of round. 192 sts.

Rounds 5–7: Work in patt.

Rep rounds 4–7 five more times, switching to 16" circular needle when necessary. 152 sts rem.

body of hat

Continue working in Miniature Herringbone Pattern without shaping (decs) for 8 rounds, ending after an odd round. You may wish to remove the markers (except the beg of round marker) for this portion of the cloche. If so, place them every 19 sts once you reach the crown.

crown

Continue in Miniature Herringbone Pattern, working the Dec Round every other row 8 times, changing to dpns when necessary. 88 sts.

Work 1 odd round even.

Dec on every round of the crown as follows:

Next round: *Work 8 sts in patt, dec (even round), work 1 st in patt; rep from * to end of round. 80 sts.

Next round: *Work 7 sts in patt, dec (odd round), work 1 st in patt; rep from * to end of round. 72 sts.

Next round: *Work 6 sts in patt, dec (even round), work 1 st in patt; rep from * to end of round. 64 sts.

Next round: *Work 5 sts in patt, dec (odd round), work 1 st in patt; rep from * to end of round. 56 sts.

Next round: *Work 4 sts in patt, dec (even round), work 1 st in patt; rep from * to end of round. 48 sts.

Next round: *Work 3 sts in patt, dec (odd round), work 1 st in patt; rep from * to end of round. 40 sts.

Next round: *Work 2 sts in patt, dec (even round), work 1 st in patt; rep from * to end of round. 32 sts.

Next round: *Work 1 sts in patt, dec (odd round), work 1 st in patt; rep from * to end of round. 24 sts.

Next round: *Dec (even round), work 1 st in patt; rep from * to end of round. 16 sts.

finishing

Cut the yarn leaving a 6" tail, and thread it through the rem 16 sts using a tapestry needle. Pull yarn gently to close the top of hat and secure the end on the WS of the hat.

Weave in ends.

ANACAPA

summery aran wrap

ANACAPA
summery aran wrap

by Kendra Nitta

The Anacapa wrap reinvents the traditional fisherman's sweater for warm climates by substituting lace for textured stitch patterns and cool hemp and cotton for Irish wool. The wrap is generously sized, and can even double as a lap blanket for two.

pattern notes

All the charts in this pattern are available for download at **www.wiley.com/go/knittinginthesun**.

directions
first half of wrap

Using scrap yarn and a provisional cast-on, CO 168 sts.

Set-up Row 1 (RS): K9, place marker (pm), k12, pm, k9, pm, *k30, pm, k9, pm, rep from * twice more, k12, pm, k9.

Set-up Row 2 (WS): K1, p7, k1, p12, k1, p7, k1, *(p1, k1) 6 times, p6, (p1, k1) 6 times, k1, p7, k1, rep from * twice more, p12, k1, p7, k1.

Begin working from the cable and lace charts as follows:

Row 1 (RS): Begin with Row 1 of each chart. Work 9 sts from Chart A; work 12 sts from Chart B; *work 9 sts from Chart C; work 30 sts from Chart D, rep from * twice more; work 9 sts from Chart C; work 12 sts from Chart E; work 9 sts from Chart F.

Continue as above working through Row 36 of all charts. Rep Rows 13–36 ten more times, then work the border.

SIZE
One size fits all

FINISHED MEASUREMENTS
Width: 27"
Length: 68"

MATERIALS
- Lanaknits Hemp for Knitting *Hempton* (40% cotton, 30% hemp, 30% modal; 130 yd. per 50g ball); color: 69 Pebble; 16 balls
- US 5 (3.75mm) circular needle, 24" length (*or size needed to match gauge*)
- Cable needle
- Stitch markers
- Scrap yarn
- Tapestry needle

GAUGE
22 sts × 30 rows = 4" in St st

SKILLS USED
increasing, decreasing, cables, following multiple charts, provisional cast-on

Key to Charts

	knit	
☐	K on RS, P on WS	

	purl	
●	P on RS, K on WS	

	s2kp	
⋀	Slip 2 sts together as if to k2tog. Knit 1 st. Pass 2 slipped sts over the st just knit	

	yo	
⊙	yarn over	

	k2tog	
╱	Knit 2 sts together as 1 st	

	ssk	
╲	Slip 1 st as if to knit, slip another st as if to knit. Insert LH needle into front of these 2 sts and knit them together	

C3F
Slip 2 sts to cable needle, hold to front, p1, k2 from cable needle

C3B
Slip 1 st to cable needle, hold to back, k2, p1 from cable needle

C6F
Slip 3 sts to cable needle, hold to front, k3, k3 from cable needle

C6B
Slip 3 sts to cable needle, hold to back, k3, k3 from cable needle

C8F
Slip 4 sts to cable needle, hold to front, k4, k4 from cable needle

C8B
Slip 4 sts to cable needle, hold to back, k4, k4 from cable needle

Chart F   Chart E

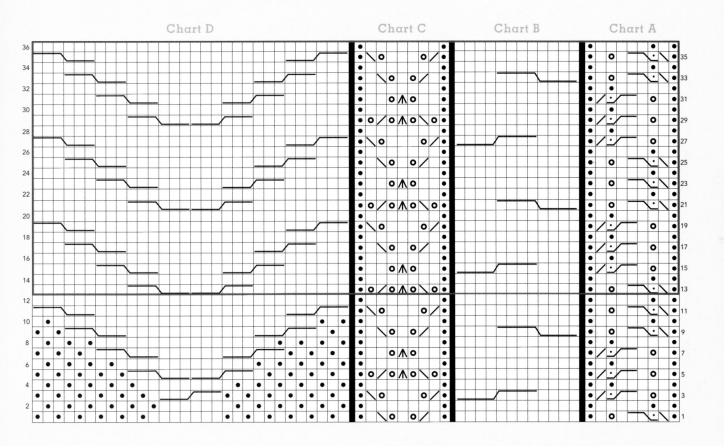

Chart D   Chart C   Chart B   Chart A

border

Row 1 (RS): P1, k1, yo, k1, C3B, k2tog, p1; *k1, p1; rep from * to last 9 sts; p1, ssk, C3F, k1, yo, k1, p1.

Row 2: K1, p5, k1, p1, *k1, p1; rep from * to last 9 sts; k1, p1, k1, p5, k1.

Row 3: P1, k1, yo, k1, C3B, k2tog, p1; k4, *s2kp, k7; rep from * to last 15 sts; s2kp, k3, p1, ssk, C3F, k1, yo, k1, p1. 138 sts.

Row 4: K1, p5, k1, p1, k to last 8 sts; p1, k1, p5, k1.

Rows 5 and 7: P1, ssk, C3F, k1, yo, k1, p1; *k1, m1, k2, s2kp, k2, m1, rep from * to last 9 sts; p1, k1, yo, k1, C3B, k2tog, p1.

Rows 6 and 8: K1, p1, k1, p5, k to last 8 sts; p5, k1, p1, k1.

To BO: Work 2 sts in patt as follows, *then bring the outside st on the RH needle over the inside st on the RH needle, work another st in patt and rep from * across: P1, ssk, C3F, k2, p1; k1, *m1, k7, m1, k1; rep from * to last 16 sts; m1, k7, m1, p1, k2, C3B, k2tog, p1. (There are no yarn overs in this row.)

second half of wrap

Remove scrap yarn from cast-on edge and place the 168 live sts on a needle. With WS facing, work Set-up Row 2 above, placing markers at every panel.

Make the second half the same as the first, beginning with Row 1 under "First Half of Wrap."

finishing

Weave in ends.

Block to measurements, gently shaping points on edges and borders.

BORDEAUX
lace shawl

BORDEAUX
lace shawl

by Janine Le Cras

This beautiful rectangular shawl, knit in a laceweight merino and silk blend, is perfect for keeping off the chill of an evening breeze or overzealous air conditioning. Named for a beach near the designer's home on the island of Guernsey, this Bordeaux wrap is perfect to carry along for any time you might need to ward off a chill in the air.

pattern notes

Work the lace charts reading odd-numbered rows from left to right and even-numbered rows from right to left.

You will work the stole in two halves and then graft it in the center.

The charts used in this pattern are available for you to download and print at **www.wiley.com/go/knittinginthesun**.

directions

CO 109 sts loosely.

Knit 3 rows to form garter st edging.

Begin Madeira Lace Chart A with Row 1, rep the 20 sts between the red lines 4 times in all before completing the row.

Work through Rows 1–34 twice (68 rows).

Work rows 69–86 from Chart B once.

SIZE
One size fits all

FINISHED MEASUREMENTS
Width: 22"

Length: 80"

MATERIALS
- Lorna's Laces *Helen's Lace* (50% silk, 50% wool; 1250 yd. per 100g skein); color: Manzanita; 1 skein
- US 4 (3.5mm) circular or straight needles *(or size needed to match gauge)*
- Stitch holders or scrap yarn
- Tapestry needle

GAUGE
24 sts × 32 rows = 4" in St st, blocked

SKILLS USED
increasing, decreasing, chart reading, grafting (Kitchener stitch)

Madeira Lace Chart B

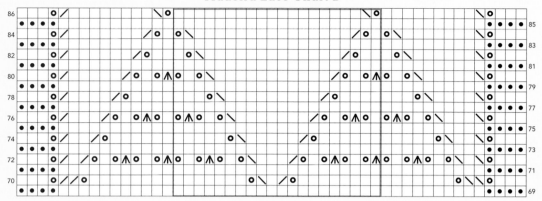

Madeira Lace Chart A

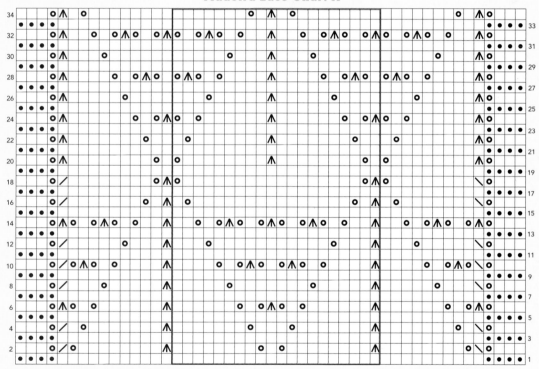

Key to Charts

	knit K on RS, P on WS		**yo** yarn over		**ssk** Slip 1 st as if to knit, slip another st as if to knit. Insert LH needle into front of these 2 sts and knit them together
	purl P on RS, K on WS		**k2tog** Knit 2 sts together as 1 st		**s2kp** Slip 2 sts together as if to k2tog. Knit 1 st. Pass 2 slipped sts over the st just knit

Rep Rows 85 and 86 only until work measures 35" unstretched, ending with Row 86.

Place all sts onto a holder or scrap yarn.

Work a second piece in the same way, ending with Row 85.

finishing

Graft the two halves of the stole together in patt, following Row 86.

Wet block the stole to the given dimensions and leave to dry. Once dry, unpin and weave in any rem ends.

SILVER STRAND
ocean waves wrap

by Dawn Leeseman

Whether you wear this light wrap to keep away a cool summer breeze or to add a touch of glamour to your outfit, the compliments are sure to follow. The beautiful openwork wave pattern is so surprisingly easy that you will want to make more than one.

pattern notes
elongated old shale pattern

(worked over multiple of 11 sts + 1)

Row 1 (RS): Knit.

Row 2 (WS): Purl.

Row 3: K1, *yo, k1, yo, k1, s2pk, k3tog, k1, yo, k1, yo, k1, rep from * to end.

Row 4: Knit.

Row 5: *K1, yo2, rep from * to last st, k1.

Row 6: Knit, letting extra wraps drop. (St count rem unchanged).

directions

CO 243 sts.

Work Rows 1–6 of Elongated Old Shale Pattern 11 times. Work Rows 1–4 once more.

BO all sts loosely.

finishing

Weave in all ends.

Block to open up the lace pattern, taking care to shape and define the scalloped edges.

SIZE
One size fits all

FINISHED MEASUREMENTS
Width: 18"

Length: 65"

MATERIALS
- Trendsetter Yarns *Serene* (35% silk, 35% cotton, 12% viscose, 10% linen, 6% lurex, 2% nylon; 115 yd. per 50g skein); color: 39 Blue Calvins; 5 skeins
- US 9 (5.5mm) circular needle, 40" length or longer (*or size needed to match gauge*)
- Tapestry needle

GAUGE
15 sts × 15 rows = 4" in Elongated Old Shale Pattern, blocked

SKILLS USED
increasing, decreasing, double yarn overs

LAGUNA
vining leaves scarf

LAGUNA
vining leaves scarf

by Eileen Adler

E ven on the warmest days, this is a handknit accessory you can wear! The vining leaves are as cool as a shady tree and can be worn in a variety of ways. A single silky vine can act as a stunning necklace, while multiple vines in a variety of yarns create an interesting, fun scarf. It also works great as a belt.

This quick knit uses a modest amount of yarn: a perfect use for that small, special skein you've been saving.

pattern notes

This pattern is appropriate for nearly any yarn. Don't be afraid to experiment! Finer yarns will yield a more delicate vine of leaves; super-bulky yarns will give you bigger, dramatic leaves.

directions

CO 5 sts using knitted cast-on.

Row 1 (RS): K2, yo, k1, yo, k2. 7 sts.

Row 2 and all even rows: Purl.

Row 3: K3, yo, k1, yo, k3. 9 sts.

Row 5: K4, yo, k1, yo, k4. 11 sts.

Row 7: K5, yo, k1, yo, k5. 13 sts.

Row 9: K5, s2kp, k5. 11 sts.

Row 11: K4, s2kp, k4. 9 sts.

Row 13: K3, s2kp, k3. 7 sts.

Row 15: K2, s2kp, k2. 5 sts.

Row 17: K1, s2kp, k1. 3 sts.

Row 19: S2kp. 1 st.

SIZE
One size fits all

FINISHED MEASUREMENTS
Width: 1½–2½", depending on yarn chosen
Length: 50"

MATERIALS

- [A] Curious Creek Fibers *Kalahari* (100% nylon; 87 yd. per 50g skein); color: Birches in Norway; 1 skein

- [B] Curious Creek Fibers *Isalo* (100% silk; 262 yd. per 95g skein); color: Birches in Norway; 1 skein

- [C] Curious Creek Fibers *Etosha* (90% kid mohair, 10% nylon; 110 yd. per 25g skein); color: Emerald City; 1 skein

- Needle size appropriate for the yarn chosen

- Tapestry needle

continued ➤

➤ continued

Row 20: Return st to LH needle and CO 4 more sts using knitted cast-on. 5 sts.

Rep Rows 1–20 until scarf measures 50", or desired length. On last leaf, end with Row 18.

Next row: K1, k2 tog. 2 sts rem.

With the 2 rem sts, work I-cord for 2".

finishing

Cut yarn leaving a 12" tail. Use a tapestry needle to bring yarn through the 2 rem sts. Pull tight to secure. Bring bound-off edge to beginning of I-cord to create a loop and sew in place. Weave in end. Block if necessary.

To wear, thread a leaf (or many leaves!) through the I-cord loop.

MONACO
driving scarf

by Katherine Vaughan

C ome summer, I envy Grace Kelly driving down the coast of Monaco with her hair held safe in a light scarf. When she reaches her destination, she either leaves the scarf on her hair or lets it pool around her shoulders. . . .

This lightweight, mesh scarf can hold back your hair or hold off an a/c-induced chill. The bamboo yarn is featherweight and noninsulating, making it a great choice for a summer scarf. With a simple lace stitch pattern, sideways construction, and pointed ends, this quick but interesting pattern will become a mainstay of any summer wardrobe—whether or not you're a movie star!

pattern notes

On even rows, work 2 sts (k1, p1) in double yo; work 1 st (k1) in single yo.

directions

CO 240 sts loosely.

Border Row 1: Knit.

Border Row 2: K1, kfb, knit to last 3 sts, k2tog, k1.

Border Row 3: Knit.

Border Row 4: K1, kfb, knit to last 3 sts, k2tog, k1.

Row 1: K2, *k2tog, yo2, ssk, rep from * to last 2 sts, k2.

Row 2: K1; kfb; knit, working [k1, p1] into each double yo, to last 3 sts; k2tog; k1.

SIZE
One size fits all

FINISHED MEASUREMENTS
Width: 6"
Length: 60"

MATERIALS
- SWTC *Bamboo* (100% bamboo; 250 yd. per 100g skein); color: 151 Lilac; 2 skeins
- US 8 (5mm) circular needle, 36" length or longer (*or size needed to match gauge*)
- Tapestry needle

GAUGE
20 sts × 32 rows = 4" in St st
Note: This is a loose gauge for this yarn.

SKILLS USED
increasing, decreasing, double yarn overs

Row 3: K3, k2tog, yo2, *ssk, k2tog, yo2, rep from * to last 7 sts, ssk, k2tog, yo, k3.

Row 4: Rep Row 2, making 2 sts in each double yo and 1 st in the single yo.

Row 5: K2, yo, *ssk, k2tog, yo2, rep from * to last 6 sts, ssk, k2tog, yo, k2.

Row 6: Rep Row 4.

Row 7: K3, yo, ssk, *k2tog, yo2, ssk, rep from * to last 3 sts, k3.

Row 8: Rep Row 4.

Rep Rows 1–8 until scarf is 5½" wide, or a half inch less than desired width.

Work Border Rows 2–4 once more.

BO all sts loosely.

finishing

Weave in ends.

Block gently.

SLEEVELESS

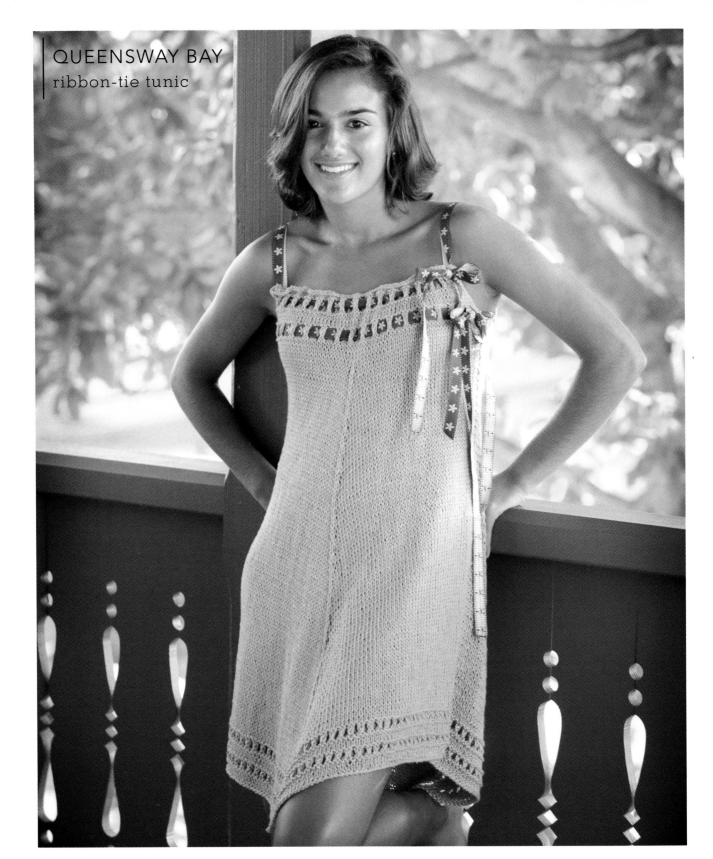

QUEENSWAY BAY

ribbon-tie tunic

by Rachel Clarke

T his lightweight tunic top is suitable for layering over pants or under a cute cardigan or bolero, offering a wide variety of possible looks and styles. If the weather is hot enough, wear it singly as a sundress on a sunny summer day. The eye-catching eyelet trim at the hem and neckline adds style and variety to the stockinette body. Easy A-line shaping and minimal seaming make this an ideal project for beginning knitters wanting to push their skills beyond simple scarves and hats. The ribbon straps woven through the neckline eyelets add contrast and allow for an adjustable custom fit with a flirty bow accent.

directions

You work the tunic in two pieces from the hem to the bodice.

front and back

(make 2)

CO 129 (145, 161, 177, 193) sts.

Row 1 (WS): Purl.

Row 2 (RS): Knit.

Row 3: Purl.

Eyelet Edging

Row 4: K 63 (71, 79, 87, 95), s2kp, k 63 (71, 79, 87, 95).

Rows 5 and 6: Knit.

Row 7 (WS): *P2tog, yo; rep from * to last st, p1.

Rows 8–10: Knit.

Row 11: Purl.

Row 12: K 62 (70, 78, 86, 94), s2kp, k 62 (70, 78, 86, 94).

Rows 13 and 14: Knit.

Row 15 (WS): *P2tog, yo; rep from * to last st, p1.

SIZE
S (M, L, 1X, 2X)

FINISHED MEASUREMENTS
Chest circumference: 32 (35, 38, 41, 45)"

To fit bust sizes up to: 34 (38, 42, 46, 50)"

Length: 29 (33, 35½, 38, 41)"

MATERIALS
- Cascade *Pima Tencel* (50% Peruvian pima cotton, 50% tencel; 109 yd. per 50g skein); color: 9501; 7 (8, 9, 11, 13) skeins
- US 8 (5mm) straight or circular needle, any length *(or size needed to match gauge) Note: The pieces are knit flat, but a circular needle might accommodate the stitches more comfortably.*
- 4 yd. of ¾"-wide ribbon
- Tapestry needle

GAUGE
18 sts × 22 rows = 4" in St st, blocked

SKILLS USED
yarn overs, double decreases

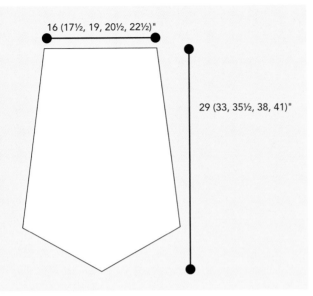

16 (17½, 19, 20½, 22½)"

29 (33, 35½, 38, 41)"

Next row (WS): *P2tog, yo; rep from * to last st, p1.

Knit 3 rows.

Purl 1 row.

Rep these 8 rows once more.

BO all sts.

finishing

Sew the two pieces together from the lower hem to the bottom of the bodice eyelets (leave the top 3" of eyelet pattern unseamed). Weave in ends. Block to measurements. Cut ribbon into 2 lengths. Weave ribbon through upper eyelets and tie as desired.

Rows 16–18: Knit.

Row 19: Purl.

Body

Row 20: K 61 (69, 77, 85, 93), s2kp, k 61 (69, 77, 85, 93).

Rows 21–23: Work in St st, starting with a purl row.

Row 24: K 60 (68, 76, 84, 92), s2kp, k 60 (68, 76, 84, 92).

Continue as set, working the double dec across the 3 center sts every fourth row 24 (30, 34, 38, 42) more times, ending with a RS row. 73 (77, 85, 93, 101) sts rem.

Bodice Eyelets

Work 3 rows in St st, starting with a purl row.

Knit 3 rows.

TAOS
convertible vest

TAOS
convertible vest
by Stefanie Japel

The Taos pattern gives you lots of options. Wear it as a tunic buttoned up the front or back, or wear it open as a vest over a blouse or T-shirt. You can also easily add length to make it a sheath dress. The waist shaping, contrasting edging, and textured stitch pattern make it a winner however you choose to wear it.

pattern notes
andalusian stitch pattern

(worked over a multiple of 2 sts + 1)

Row 1 (RS): Knit.

Row 2 (WS): Purl.

Row 3: *K1, p1; rep from * to last st, k1.

Row 4: Purl.

Rep these 4 rows for patt.

seed stitch pattern

(worked on an odd number of sts)

All rows: K1, *p1, k1, rep from * to end.

decreases

On RS rows: Decrease with k1, ssk at the beginning of rows and k2tog, k1 at the end of rows.

On WS rows: Decrease with p1, ssp at the beginning of rows and p2tog, p1 at the end of rows.

SIZE
XS (S, M, L, 1X, 2X, 3X)

FINISHED MEASUREMENTS
Chest circumference: 31 (35, 39, 43, 47, 51, 55)"

Length: 31 (31, 33, 33, 34½, 34½, 34½)"

MATERIALS
- Berroco *Love-it* (58% cotton, 38% acrylic, 4% polyester; 120 yd. per 50g ball); MC: 3207 Sagebrush, 9 (10, 11, 12, 13, 14, 15) balls; CC: 3228 Brownstone, 1 (1, 1, 1, 1, 1, 1) ball
- US 8 (5mm) straight or circular needles (*or size needed to match gauge*)
- US 6 (4mm) straight or circular needles
- Tapestry needle

GAUGE
18 sts × 24 rows = 4" in Andalusian Stitch Pattern on larger needles

SKILLS USED
increasing, decreasing, picking up stitches

directions

The vest is worked in the Andalusian Stitch Pattern throughout.

back

Using larger needles and MC, CO 79 (85, 95, 101, 111, 121, 129) sts.

Work in Andalusian Stitch Pattern for 7½ (8, 8½, 8½, 9, 9½, 9½)", ending with a WS row. If you would like a longer vest, add length here, before you begin the shaping.

Shape Waist

Dec 1 st at each end of the next row, and every following 4th (5th, 4th, 6th, 6th, 4th, 5th) row 8 (7, 8, 6, 6, 7, 6) more times. 61 (69, 77, 87, 97, 117, 115) sts.

Work even for 14 (10, 14, 8, 12, 16, 14) rows.

Inc 1 st at each end of the next row, and then every following 6th (7th, 7th, 7th, 9th, 6th, 8th) row 5 (5, 5, 5, 4, 5, 4) more times. 73 (81, 89, 99, 107, 117, 125) sts.

Work even until piece measures 23 (23, 24½, 25, 25½, 25, 25)" from hem.

Shape Armhole

BO 6 (6, 7, 7, 8, 9, 9) sts at the beg of next 2 rows. 61 (69, 75, 85, 91, 99, 107) sts.

Dec 1 st at each end every RS row 1 (1, 1, 1, 1, 2, 2) time(s). 59 (67, 73, 83, 89, 95, 103) sts rem.

Divide for Neck and Continue with Armhole Shaping

Work 27 (31, 34, 39, 42, 45, 49) sts. With a second ball of yarn, BO center 5 sts, work remaining 27 (31, 34, 39, 42, 45, 49) sts.

Working each side separately, dec 1 st at armhole edges every RS row 3 (6, 7, 9, 11, 11, 13) times more, then shape neck. 24 (25, 27, 30, 31, 34, 36) sts on each side.

Shape Neck

Dec 1 st at neck edge of next row, then every other row 10 (14, 15, 10, 9, 13, 14) times, then every 4th row 3 (0, 0, 2, 2, 0, 0) times. 10 (10, 11, 13, 12, 14, 15) sts rem.

Work even until 48 (50, 52, 54, 56, 58, 64) rows are complete from beg of armhole shaping.

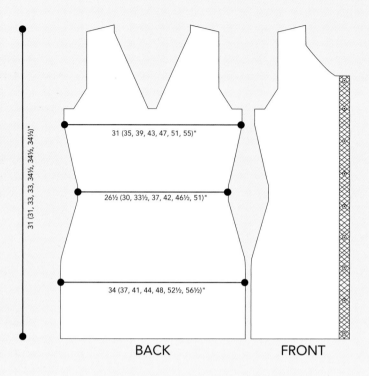

31 (31, 33, 33, 34½, 34½, 34½)"

31 (35, 39, 43, 47, 51, 55)"

26½ (30, 33½, 37, 42, 46½, 51)"

34 (37, 41, 44, 48, 52½, 56½)"

BACK

FRONT

Shape Shoulder

BO 5 (5, 5, 6, 6, 7, 7) sts at armhole edge.

Work 1 row even.

BO rem 5 (5, 6, 7, 6, 7, 8) sts at armhole edge.

right front

Using larger needles and MC, CO 39 (41, 47, 49, 55, 59, 63) sts.

Work in Andalusian Stitch Pattern for 7½ (8, 8½, 8½, 9, 9½, 9½)", ending with a WS row. If you would like a longer vest, add length here, before you begin the shaping.

Shape Waist

Dec 1 st at outside edge of next row, then every following 4th (4th, 4th, 6th, 6th, 4th, 5th) row 7 (7, 8, 6, 5, 7, 6) times to 30 (33, 38, 42, 48, 51, 56) sts.

Work even for 8 (4, 11, 3, 2, 12, 8) more rows.

Inc 1 st at outside edge of next row, then every following 6th (7th, 7th, 7th, 9th, 6th, 8th) row 5 (5, 5, 5, 4, 5, 4) times to 36 (39, 44, 48, 53, 57, 61) sts.

Work even for 10 (10, 12, 12, 12, 12, 12) more rows.

Shape Armhole

BO 6 (6, 7, 7, 8, 9, 9) sts at armhole edge.

Dec 1 st at armhole every RS row 4 (7, 8, 10, 12, 13, 14) times.

Continue until 20 (22, 22, 24, 26, 26, 28) rows have been worked from beg of armhole shaping. 26 (26, 29, 31, 33, 35, 38) sts rem.

Shape Neck

BO 4 (4, 6, 5, 6, 6, 6) sts at neck edge.

Dec 1 st at neck edge every row 5 (6, 6, 6, 7, 7, 8) times, then dec 1 st at neck edge every other row 6 (6, 6, 7, 8, 8, 8) times until 10 (10, 11, 13, 12, 14, 15) sts rem.

Work even until 48 (50, 52, 54, 56, 58, 64) rows have been worked from beg of armhole shaping.

Shape Shoulder

BO 5 (5, 5, 6, 6, 7, 7) sts at armhole edge.

Work 1 row even.

BO rem 5 (5, 6, 7, 6, 7, 8) sts at armhole edge.

left front

Work as for Right Front, reversing shaping.

finishing

button band

Using smaller needles and MC, pick up and knit 117 (117, 125, 125, 127, 127, 129) sts (approximately 3 sts for every 4 rows along left front) between bottom of hem and bottom of neckline).

Work in Seed Stitch for 7 rows. BO loosely.

Mark positions for 9 buttons, the first one ½" above the band bottom, the last one ½" below the band top. You should evenly space the rest between these two, approximately 3" apart.

buttonhole band

Work buttonhole band as for button band, working buttonholes as follows:

On Row 4, *work in Seed Stitch to the buttonhole marker, (yo, k2tog), rep from * to last marker, finishing the row in Seed Stitch. Work Rows 5–7 in Seed Stitch. BO loosely.

picot trim

Work picot trim around neckline, armholes, and hem. To do so, mark the edges every 2". Using CC and larger needles, pick up and knit 9 sts between each set of markers (or 4½ sts per inch), being sure to pick up an odd number of sts. Work the edgings back and forth on these sts as follows.

Row 1: Purl.

Row 2: Knit.

Row 3: P1, *yo, p2tog, rep from * to end.

Row 4: Knit.

Row 5: Purl.

BO. Fold edging to inside along eyelet row. Sew the bound-off edge to the picked-up edge, completing trim.

Finish by sewing side and shoulder seams. Attach buttons opposite the buttonholes. Weave in rem ends.

LUDINGTON
smocked tube-top

by Amy Polcyn

This flirty tube top is worked in the round and is within the grasp of any knitter, including adventurous beginners. The smocking stitch creates a wonderful texture but is deceptively easy to knit. The cotton-blend yarn has plenty of stretch to keep the top in place; encased elastic leaves you worry-free to enjoy your day in the sun.

pattern notes

The smocked bodice is worked in the round from the bottom up; the lower portion of tunic is picked up from bodice and worked from the top down.

Select a yarn with sufficient elasticity to ensure a proper fit; a 100% cotton yarn may not give satisfactory results.

smocking stitch pattern

(worked in the round on a multiple of 8 sts)

Rounds 1–3: *K2, p2; rep from * around.

Round 4: *Insert the right needle, from front to back, between 6th and 7th st on left needle, wrap yarn around needle and pull up a loop, place loop on left needle, knit this new loop together with the next st on the needle as k2tog, k1, p2, k2, p2; rep from * around.

Rounds 5–7: *K2, p2; rep from * around.

Round 8: K2, p2, *insert right needle, from front to back, between 6th and 7th st on left needle, wrap yarn around needle and pull up a loop, place the loop on the left needle and knit this new loop together with the next st on the needle as k2tog, k1, p2, k2, p2; rep from * to last 4 sts, insert right needle between the 2nd and 3rd sts after the marker, wrap yarn and pull up a loop as before and knit it together with the next st on the needle, k1, p2. Do not move marker.

Rep Rounds 1–8 for patt.

SIZE
Women's XS (S, M, L, 1X, 2X, 3X)

FINISHED MEASUREMENTS
Chest circumference: 30 (34, 38, 42, 46, 50, 54)"
Length: 19 (20, 21, 22, 23, 24, 25)"

MATERIALS
- Nashua Handknits *Cilantro* (70% cotton, 30% polyester; 136 yd. per 50g ball); color: 017 Turquoise; 8 (9, 10, 11, 12, 13, 14) balls
- US 8 (5mm) circular needle, 24" and 36" lengths (*or size needed to match gauge*)
- 1 (1, 1½, 1½, 1½, 1½, 1¾) yd. elastic, ½" wide
- Large safety pin
- Sewing needle and thread to match yarn
- Stitch markers
- Tapestry needle

GAUGE
20 sts × 28 rows = 4" in St st
22 sts × 28 rows = 4" in Smocking Stitch Pattern, slightly stretched

SKILLS USED
knitting in the round, increasing, unusual stitch pattern

directions

bodice

You will begin with the smocked bodice, working from bottom to top.

With 24" circular needle, CO 152 (176, 200, 216, 240, 264, 280) sts. Place marker (pm) and join in the round, being careful not to twist sts.

Work in Smocking Stitch Pattern for 9 (9½, 10, 10½, 11, 11½, 12)", ending with Round 2 or Round 6.

Next round: Purl to create a turning ridge.

Work in k2, p2 rib for 1" to create casing to conceal the elastic.

BO loosely, using a larger needle if necessary.

skirt

With 24" circular needle, pick up and knit 150 (170, 190, 210, 230, 250, 270) sts around lower edge of bodice (the cast-on edge). Place marker and join to knit in the round.

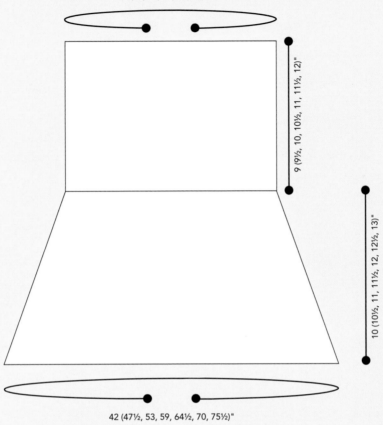

30 (34, 38, 42, 46, 50, 54)"

9 (9½, 10, 10½, 11, 11½, 12)"

10 (10½, 11, 11½, 12, 12½, 13)"

42 (47½, 53, 59, 64½, 70, 75½)"

Rounds 1–7: Knit.

Round 8: *K5, m1; rep from * around.
180 (204, 228, 252, 276, 300, 324) sts.

Change to longer circular needle when needed.

Rounds 9–15: Knit.

Round 16: *K6, m1; rep from * around.
210 (238, 266, 294, 322, 350, 378) sts.

Work even until lower portion measures 10
(10½, 11, 11½, 12, 12½, 13)", or desired length.

Next round: Purl to create a turning ridge for
the hem facing.

Knit 8 more rounds for hem facing.

BO loosely.

finishing

Turn up hem along purl ridges. Stitch in place.

Fold down casing along purl ridges. Stitch,
matching sts and being careful not to work too
tightly. The casing needs to stretch comfortably
when worn. Leave a 1½" opening. Do not cut
yarn. Cut elastic approximately 2" longer than
bust measurement. Attach safety pin to one end
of elastic and feed through casing. Adjust the
fit; overlap ends of the elastic and secure with
needle and thread. Sew the rest of the casing
closed. Weave in ends.

ANNA MARIA
hourglass shell
by Carol Feller

C ool bamboo is a delight to wear in warmer weather. This flattering, form-fitting shell is designed to hug your curves while the gently shaped hourglass-stitch patterning echoes these lines. The result is a very feminine top you can wear anywhere. For cooler days and more versatility, try it paired with the Quimper bolero on page 111.

pattern notes

This shell is knit from the bottom up in the round.

This top is meant to have a body-conscious fit. Knit this shell to your bust measurement or an inch or two smaller for the proper fit.

The charts used in this pattern are available for you to download and print at **www.wiley.com/go/knittinginthesun**.

seed stitch pattern

(worked over an even number of sts in the round)

Round 1: (K1, p1) rep to end of round.

Round 2: (P1, k1) rep to end of round.

Rep these 2 rounds for Seed Stitch.

directions

Using smaller circular needle, CO 176 (200, 228, 252, 276, 300, 328) sts, place marker (pm), and join to work in the round, being careful not to twist sts.

Work in Seed Stitch for 6 rounds.

You will work waist and bust shaping at the same time as you knit the Hourglass Chart patterns. Read through this section completely before continuing.

SIZE

XS (S, M, L, 1X, 2X, 3X)

FINISHED MEASUREMENTS

Chest circumference: 30 (34, 38, 42, 46, 50, 54)"

Length: 21½ (22, 22½, 23, 23½, 24, 25)"

MATERIALS

- Rowan *Bamboo Soft* (100% bamboo; 112 yd. per 50g ball); color: 109 Cambria; 6 (6, 7, 8, 8, 9, 10) balls
- US 5 (3.75mm) circular needle, 24" or 36" length *(or size needed to match gauge)*
- US 4 (3.5mm) circular needle, 24" or 36" length
- US 4 (3.5mm) double-pointed needles
- 12 stitch markers: 8 of one sort, 4 contrasting
- Tapestry needle

continued ➤

➤ continued

GAUGE

24 sts × 32 rows = 4" in St st on larger needles, unblocked

24 sts × 30 rows = 4" in St st on larger needles, blocked

SKILLS USED

knitting in the round, increasing, decreasing, chart reading, following shaping and pattern instructions simultaneously

Change to larger circular needle.

On Round 1, you will place markers to position the 4 shaping darts and the 4 hourglass pattern panels. Use contrasting colors to differentiate the dart markers from the chart markers that you are putting in place.

NOTE Work the shaping portions for the Waist and the Bust while you work through the row-by-row instructions for the hourglass chart panels.

SHAPE WAIST

Work 6 (4, 3, 3, 3, 4, 3) rounds in Hourglass patt.

Next round: Work to 2 sts before the first dart marker, k2tog, slip marker (sm), work to second dart marker and slip it, ssk, work to 2 sts before third dart marker, k2tog, sm, work to fourth dart marker and slip it, ssk, work to end of round. 172 (196, 224, 248, 272, 296, 324) sts.

Rep these 7 (5, 4, 4, 4, 5, 4) rounds 5 (7, 8, 8, 8, 7, 8) times. 152 (168, 192, 216, 240, 268, 292) sts.

Round 1: *Work the 19 sts from the Triple Hourglass Chart, place chart marker, k 6 (8, 9, 9, 9, 8, 9), place dart marker, k 19 (23, 29, 35, 41, 48, 54), place chart marker, work 19 sts from chart, place chart marker, k 19 (23, 29, 35, 41, 48, 54), place dart marker, k 6 (8, 9, 9, 9, 8, 9), place chart marker, rep from *. 12 markers placed.

Rounds 2–16: Work 2 reps of the Triple Hourglass Chart and, *at the same time,* begin waist shaping (see above).

On the last round of the second repeat of the Triple Hourglass chart, move both markers in 3 sts on each side of the patt panels. Each panel is now 13 sts wide and the beg of round marker has been moved over 3 sts.

Round 17: *Work first round of the Double Hourglass Chart over 13 sts, p1, k to 1 st before next patt panel, p1, rep from * around.

Rounds 18–32: Continue to work 2 reps of the Double Hourglass Chart and shaping the waist as set.

On the last round of the second repeat of the Double Hourglass Chart, move both markers in 3 sts on each side of the patt panels. Each panel is now 7 sts wide and the beg of round marker has been moved over 3 sts.

Triple Hourglass Chart

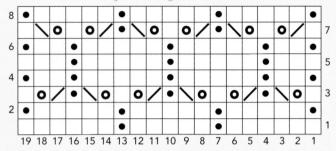

Double Hourglass Chart

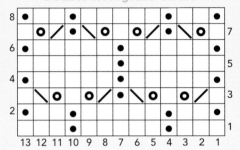

Single Hourglass Chart

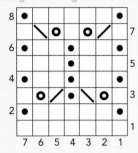

Key to Hourglass Charts

knit
K on RS, P on WS

purl
P on RS, K on WS

yo
yarn over

k2tog
Knit 2 sts together as 1 st

ssk
Slip 1 st as if to knit, slip another st as if to knit. Insert LH needle into front of these 2 sts and knit them together

Rounds 33: *Work the first round of the Single Hourglass Chart over 7 sts, p1, k to 1 st before next patt panel, p1, rep from * around.

Rounds 34-48: Continue to work 2 reps of the Single Hourglass Chart. Complete the waist shaping and work even through Round 48.

Rounds 49–72 (Rounds 49–80 for sizes 2X and 3X): Begin bust shaping (see below) as you work 3 (3, 3, 3, 4, 4) more reps of the Single Hourglass Chart.

On the last round, move both markers out 3 sts on each side of the patt panels. Each panel is now 13 sts wide.

Next round: Work to first dart marker, M1L, work to second dart marker and slip it, M1R, work to third marker, M1L, work to fourth marker and slip it, M1R, work to end of round. 4 sts increased.

Work 5 (4, 3, 3, 3, 4, 3) rounds in patt.

Rep these 6 (5, 4, 4, 4, 5, 4) rounds 5 (7, 8, 8, 8, 7, 8) times. 176 (200, 228, 252, 276, 300, 328) sts.

Rounds 73–88 (Rounds 81–96 for sizes 2X and 3X): Work 2 reps of the Double Hourglass Chart and continue with shaping; on the first round, bet each set of patt panel markers, k2, p1, work 7 sts from chart, p1, k2.

On the last round, move both markers out 3 sts on each side of the patt panels. Each panel is now 19 sts wide.

Rounds 89–104 (Rounds 97–112 for sizes 2X and 3X): Work 2 reps of Triple Hourglass Chart. On the first round, bet each set of patt panel markers, k2, p1, work 13 sts from chart, p1, k2.

Continue with Triple Hourglass patt without shaping to end of pattern reps or until piece measures 13½ (13½, 13½, 13¾, 14, 14¼, 15)", ending on an even round of the patt rep.

SHAPE ARMHOLES AND NECK

Work the armholes and neckline at the same time. Armhole bind-offs will be centered on the side pattern panels.

K 4 (1, 0, 0, 0, 0, 0) sts, BO 11 (17, 20, 22, 24, 26, 28) sts, work 77 (83, 93, 101, 109, 117, 127) sts in patt, BO 11 (17, 21, 25, 29, 33, 37) sts, work 77 (83, 93, 101, 109, 117, 127) sts in patt, BO 0 (0, 1, 3, 5, 7, 9) sts. Cut yarn and secure.

You will now work the front and back separately. Remember to read charts appropriately for knitting back and forth.

back

NOTE Work all armhole decs 1 st in from the edge. At the beg of a row, use k1, ssk (for RS) or p1, p2tog (for WS). At the end of a row, dec with k2tog, k1 (for RS) or ssp, p1 (for WS).

Working on the 77 (83, 93, 101, 109, 117, 127) sts for the Back only, continue working the Triple Hourglass Chart as established and, *at the same time,* dec 1 stitch at each armhole every row 5 (6, 8, 10, 12, 14, 15) times. 67 (71, 77, 81, 85, 89, 97) sts.

Dec 1 st at each armhole every RS row 4 (5, 4, 3, 2, 1, 0) time(s). 59 (61, 69, 75, 81, 87, 97) sts; end with a WS row.

Next row: K 9 (9, 13, 14, 17, 18, 23), BO center 41 (43, 43, 47, 47, 51, 51) sts for neck, work to end of row.

Continue with each shoulder separately.

Dec at armhole edge every RS row 0 (0, 4, 5, 8, 9, 14) more times. There are 9 sts for each shoulder.

Straps
On next RS row: K1, work 7 sts from Single Hourglass Chart, k1.

Next row (WS): P1, work Single Hourglass Chart, p1.

Continue with chart as set until armhole measures 6½ (7, 7½, 7¾, 8, 8¼, 8½)" from beg of armhole shaping.

BO all sts in patt.

front

There are 77 (83, 93, 101, 109, 117, 127) sts for the Front.

Continue working from the Triple Hourglass Chart as set and, *at the same time,* dec 1 st as for back at each armhole every row 5 times. 67 (73, 83, 91, 99, 107, 117) sts.

Work 13 (15, 20, 22, 26, 28, 33) sts, BO center 41 (43, 43, 47, 47, 51, 51) st for neck, work to end of row.

Continue with each shoulder separately.

Dec at armhole edge every row 0 (1, 3, 5, 7, 9, 10) more times. 13 (14, 17, 17, 19, 19, 23) sts on each shoulder.

Dec at armhole edge every RS row 4 (5, 8, 8, 10, 10, 14) times. There are 9 sts for each shoulder.

Finish straps as for Back.

finishing

Sew shoulders together.

neck edging

Using smaller circular needle, beg at right back shoulder, pick up and knit 41 (43, 43, 47, 47, 51, 51) sts along back neck, pm, pick up and knit 22 (26, 30, 32, 34, 36, 37) sts from back left side, pick up and knit 34 (36, 40, 42, 44, 46, 48) sts down front left side, pm, pick up and knit 41 (43, 43, 47, 47, 51, 51) sts along front neck, pm, pick up and knit 34 (36, 40, 42, 44, 46, 48) sts up front right side, pick up and knit 22 (26, 30, 32, 34, 36, 37) sts from back right side, pm to indicate beg of round.

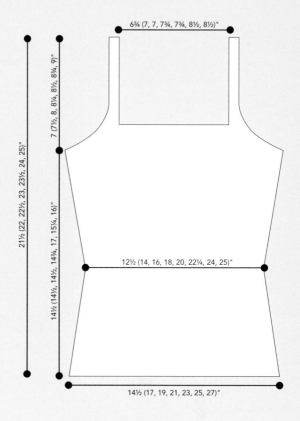

6¾ (7, 7, 7¾, 7¾, 8½, 8½)"

7 (7½, 8, 8¼, 8½, 8¾, 9)"

21½ (22, 22½, 23, 23½, 24, 25)"

14½ (14½, 14½, 14¾, 17, 15¼, 16)"

12½ (14, 16, 18, 20, 22¼, 24, 25)"

14½ (17, 19, 21, 23, 25, 27)"

Round 1: Work in Seed Stitch to end.

Dec round: *K2tog, work Seed Stitch to 2 sts before marker, ssk, repeat from * 3 more times.

Repeat these 2 rounds twice more.

BO in patt.

armhole edging

Using dpns, pick up and knit 96 (108, 120, 128, 138, 146, 156) sts around armhole, pm to indicate beg of round.

Work 5 rounds of Seed Stitch.

BO in patt.

Weave in ends.

PROVENCE

split-leaf shell

by Janine Le Cras

The name for this tank is inspired by the color. It immediately reminded me of the lavender fields that coat the Provence region of France. You can wear it on a sun-drenched country stroll or to the office worn under a structured jacket, where you might daydream of an afternoon in the South of France.

pattern notes

This top is designed to be form fitting. Choose the size that is closest to your actual chest measurement or slightly smaller.

directions

back

CO 74 (86, 98, 110, 122, 134) sts.

Begin working from Split Leaf Chart with Row 1, a RS row. Work 7 sts from chart, rep the 12 sts within the red lines 5 (6, 7, 8, 9, 10) times, work to end of chart. Continue working from chart until all 30 rows are complete, then begin waist shaping.

Shape Waist

The rest of the piece is worked in St st.

Work 3 rows even, ending with a WS row.

Next Row (Dec Row): K1, ssk, k to last 3 sts, k2tog, k1.

Continue in St st, repeating the Dec Row every 4th row 3 more times. 66 (78, 90, 102, 114, 126) sts.

Work 7 rows without shaping.

Next Row (Inc Row): K1, m1, k to last 2 sts, m1, k1.

Rep the Inc Row every 6th row 5 more times. 78 (90, 102, 114, 126, 138) sts.

Continue working without shaping until piece measures 14½ (14½, 13½, 13½, 13½, 13½)".

SIZE

XS (S, M, L, 1X, 2X)

FINISHED MEASUREMENTS

Chest circumference: 28 (33, 37, 41½, 46, 50)"

Length: 22 (23, 23, 24, 24½, 25)"

MATERIALS

- Rowan *Calmer* (75% cotton, 25% microfiber; 175 yd. per 50g ball); color: 482 Powder Puff; 3 (3, 4, 4, 5, 5) balls
- US 7 (4.5mm) straight or circular needles, any length (*or size needed to match gauge*)
- Scrap yarn or stitch holder
- Tapestry needle

GAUGE

22 sts × 32 rows = 4" in St st

SKILLS USED

increasing, decreasing, following charts

Split Leaf Chart

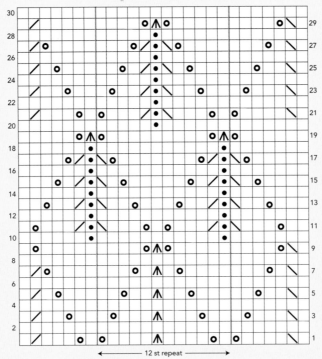

← 12 st repeat →

Key to Split Leaf Chart

	knit K on RS, P on WS		yo yarn over		ssk Slip 1 st as if to knit, slip another st as if to knit. Insert LH needle into front of these 2 sts and knit them together
☐		⊙		⊠	

	purl P on RS, K on WS		k2tog Knit 2 sts together as 1 st		s2kp Slip 2 sts together as if to k2tog. Knit 1 st. Pass 2 slipped sts over the st just knit
⊡		⧄		⋀	

Shape Armholes

BO 3 (4, 6, 7, 9, 11) sts at beg of next 2 rows.

BO 1 (2, 3, 3, 4, 5) st(s) at beg of next 2 rows.

Dec 1 st at each end of the following 1 (2, 2, 4, 5, 6) RS row(s).

Continue to work the rem 68 (74, 80, 86, 90, 96) sts until work measures 7½ (8½, 9½, 10½, 11, 11½)", then shape shoulders.

Shape Shoulders

BO 6 (7, 8, 9, 10, 11) sts at beg of next 2 rows.

BO 6 (7, 8, 9, 9, 10) sts at beg of next 2 rows.

BO 6 (7, 8, 8, 9, 10) sts at beg of next 2 rows.

BO the rem 32 (32, 32, 34, 34, 34) sts.

front

Work the front the same as the back through the armhole shaping.

When the front measures 2 (2½, 3½, 4, 4½, 4½)" from the beg of armhole shaping, divide for V-neck.

Knit 34 (37, 40, 43, 45, 48) sts. Place rem 34 (37, 40, 43, 45, 48) sts on scrap yarn or a st holder.

Shape Left Neck and Shoulder
Next RS row (Dec Row): K to last 3 sts, k2tog, k1.

Continue in St st and rep the Dec Row every RS row 7 (7, 7, 8, 8, 8) more times, then every 4th row 8 (8, 8, 8, 8, 8) times. 18 (21, 24, 26, 28, 31) sts.

Work even until armhole measures 7½ (8½, 9½, 10½, 11, 11½)", then shape shoulder.

BO 6 (7, 8, 9, 10, 11) sts at beg of next RS row.

BO 6 (7, 8, 9, 9, 10) sts at beg of next RS row.

BO 6 (7, 8, 8, 9, 10) sts at beg of next RS row.

Shape Right Neck and Shoulder
Return the held sts to the working needle, rejoin yarn at neck edge, and work 2 rows even.

Next RS row (Dec Row): K1, ssk, k to end of row.

Rep the Dec Row every RS row 7 (7, 7, 8, 8, 8) more times, then every 4th row 8 (8, 8, 8, 8, 8) times. 18 (21, 24, 26, 28, 31) sts.

Work even until armhole measures 7½ (8½, 9½, 10½, 11, 11½)", then shape shoulder.

BO 6 (7, 8, 9, 10, 11) sts at beg of next WS row.

BO 6 (7, 8, 9, 9, 10) sts at beg of next WS row.

BO 6 (7, 8, 8, 9, 10) sts at beg of next WS row.

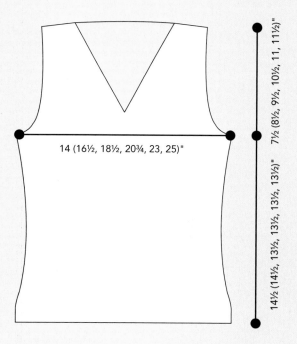

14 (16½, 18½, 20¾, 23, 25)"

7½ (8½, 9½, 10½, 11, 11½)"

14½ (14½, 13½, 13½, 13½, 13½)"

finishing

Block the pieces to the given measurements.

Sew the right shoulder seam.

neck edging

Starting at the top of the left front, with the RS facing pick up and knit 36 (39, 39, 42, 42, 44) sts down the left front, 36 (39, 39, 42, 42, 44) sts up the right front, and 32 (32, 32, 34, 34, 34) sts across the back. Knit 1 row. BO all sts.

Sew up rem shoulder seam.

armhole edging

With RS facing, pick up and knit 66 (72, 88, 90, 96,100) sts along armhole edge. Knit 1 row. BO all sts.

Work second armhole the same.

Sew up the side seams and weave in ends.

SHORT SLEEVES

AVIARA
ruffled surplice top

by Marnie MacLean

Ocean towns are prized not only for their spectacular views, but also for their temperate climate. The ocean serves to regulate the temperature and the breezes are a refreshing respite from the blazing sun. As the sun sets, that same breeze can bring a little chill to bare shoulders. Aviara offers the coolness of linen with a bit of insulating wool and alpaca to keep out the breeze, while the ruffles add a feminine flourish to the practical piece. You can wear this short-sleeved top as a casual layered element, perfect for a late evening stroll to watch the sun set, or dress it up with a skirt and lace camisole to wear to dinner and a show. This versatile and flattering piece suits a variety of shapes and sizes.

pattern notes

The front panels of this top are not quite as wide as the back; this makes it possible to get a perfect fit. Knit a size larger if you are between sizes.

If you prefer a less revealing neckline, work fewer decreases before beginning the front straps to make them wider. Make sure to adjust the back neck bind-off so the shoulder stitches for the back match the number of stitches in the front.

Slip the first stitch of each row purlwise to create a smooth edge and to make working the crocheted edging easier.

directions
body

The body begins with a provisional cast-on and is worked in one piece in St st. Later, you will pick up the stitches from the provisional cast-on and knit the ruffle.

Using a provisional cast-on and 24" circular needle, CO 174 (199, 225, 250, 276, 301, 327, 351) sts. Place markers 55 (63, 72, 80, 89, 97, 106, 114) sts in from each end to separate the fronts and the back.

SIZE
XS (S, M, L, 1X, 2X, 3X, 4X)

FINISHED MEASUREMENTS
Chest circumference: 30 (34, 38, 42, 46, 50, 54, 58)"

Length: 24 (24¾, 25, 25¾, 26, 26¾, 27, 27¾)"

MATERIALS
- Classic Elite Yarns *Soft Linen* (35% wool, 35% linen, 30% baby alpaca; 137 yd. per 50g ball); color: 2225 Smoky Rose; 6 (7, 8, 9, 9, 10, 11, 12) balls

- US 6 (4mm) circular needle, 24" length, or longer for larger sizes *(or size needed to match gauge)*

- US 6 (4mm) circular needle, 12" length

- US 6 (4mm) double-pointed needles

- US E (3.5mm) crochet hook

continued ➤

➤ continued

- 2 stitch markers
- Stitch holders or scrap yarn
- Tapestry needle
- 5' length of 1½" wide organza ribbon
- 2' length of ¼" wide ribbon
- Sewing needle
- Thread to match garment

GAUGE

22 sts × 28 rows = 4" in St st

SKILLS USED

increasing, decreasing, short-row shaping, knitting in the round, single crochet, double crochet, three-needle bind-off, following shaping and pattern instructions simultaneously

Shape Waist

Working in St st and remembering to slip the first st of every row, dec every 6 (6, 6, 5, 6, 5, 6, 5) rows 3 (7, 3, 1, 3, 2, 3, 3) times, then every 7 (0, 7, 6, 7, 6, 7, 6) rows 4 (0, 3, 5, 2, 3, 1, 1) time(s), working dec as follows:

> *On RS rows: Sl 1, *k to 2 sts before marker, k2tog, slip marker (sm), ssk. Rep from *, then work to end of row.*

> *On WS rows: Sl 1, *p to 2 sts before marker, ssp, sm, p2tog. Rep from *, then work to end of row.*

Work 7 rows even for waist. There are 48 (56, 65, 73, 83, 91, 100, 109) sts for each front and 50 (59, 67, 76, 86, 95, 103, 113) sts for the back. 146 (171, 197, 222, 252, 277, 303, 331) sts total.

You will work the decreases to shape the front neck at the same time as the bust shaping. When the bust shaping is complete, you will continue with the neck shaping and begin the armhole shaping. Please read the sections on neck and bust and armhole shaping before continuing and use the schematic as a reference for construction.

Shape Neck

(Work at the same time as bust and armhole shaping)

Begin neckline shaping immediately after the 7 rows for the waist.

BO 4 sts at beg of next 2 rows.

Dec every RS row 11 (12, 13, 14, 16, 17, 18, 19) times, then every row 29 (34, 39, 44, 47, 52, 57, 62) times, working dec as follows:

> *On RS rows: Sl 1, ssk, work to last 3 sts, k2tog, k1.*

> *On WS rows: Sl 1, p2tog, work to last 3 sts, ssp, p1.*

SHAPE BUST AND ARMHOLE
(WORK AT THE SAME TIME AS NECK SHAPING)

*Work Inc rows as follows: Dec at neckline if required; *work to 1 st before marker, m1, work 2 sts in St st, m1, rep from * 1 more time; work to end of row, shaping neckline edge as required.*

Inc on the next row, then inc every 4 (5, 5, 5, 6, 6, 7, 7) rows 4 (8, 5, 1, 6, 2, 7, 3) times, then every 5 (0, 6, 6, 7, 7, 8, 8) rows 4 (0, 3, 7, 2, 6, 1, 5) times. 68 (77, 85, 94, 104, 113, 121, 131) sts for back between the two markers.

When the piece measures 13" (for all sizes), begin armhole shaping.

Maintain patt as set to 2 (2, 3, 5, 5, 6, 7, 7) sts before marker; BO 4 (4, 6, 10, 10, 12, 14, 14) sts, removing the marker. Rep at second marker. Work to end of row in patt.

You will now work the right front, the back, and the left front separately.

left and right fronts

Dec at armhole edge every RS row 4 (6, 7, 7, 10, 11, 12, 15) times. On the right front, end dec rows with k2tog, k1. On the left front, begin dec rows with k1, ssk.

At the same time, continue with the neckline shaping as directed above until 7 (7, 8, 8, 9, 9, 10, 10) sts rem for the shoulder straps.

Work even for 4½" more (for all sizes).

back

Dec at armhole edges every RS row 4 (6, 7, 7, 10, 11, 12, 15) times. Work Dec Rows as follows: k1, ssk, k to last 3 sts, k2tog, k1.

Work even until the back measures 16½ (17, 17¼, 18, 18¼, 18½, 19, 19½)".

BO center 34 (39, 41, 46, 48, 53, 55, 59) sts.

Dec every row at the neckline edge for 7 rows. 7 (7, 8, 8, 9, 9, 10, 10) sts for each shoulder.

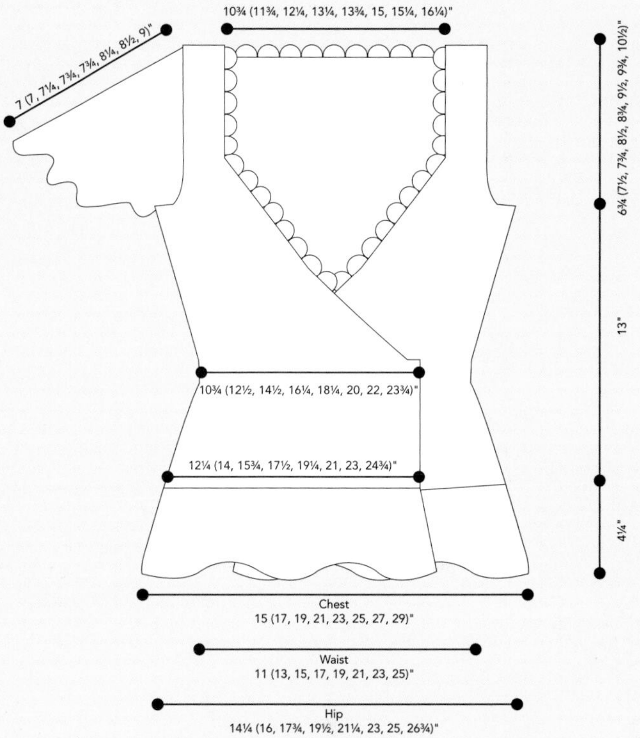
10¾ (11¾, 12¼, 13¼, 13¾, 15, 15¼, 16¼)"
7 (7, 7¼, 7¾, 7¾, 8¼, 8½, 9)"
6¾ (7½, 7¾, 8½, 8¾, 9½, 9¾, 10½)"
13"
4¼"
10¾ (12½, 14½, 16¼, 18¼, 20, 22, 23¾)"
12¼ (14, 15¾, 17½, 19¼, 21, 23, 24¾)"
Chest
15 (17, 19, 21, 23, 25, 27, 29)"
Waist
11 (13, 15, 17, 19, 21, 23, 25)"
Hip
14¼ (16, 17¾, 19½, 21¼, 23, 25, 26¾)"

Turn garment inside out and match up shoulder straps for front and back. Use the three-needle bind-off (see the "Special Knitting Techniques" appendix) to attach the shoulder straps. Cut yarn and secure by pulling tail through the last loop.

bottom ruffle

Remove the provisional cast-on and place sts on the longer circular needle. (For larger sizes, use a longer needle to accommodate the sts.) 174 (199, 225, 250, 276, 301, 327, 351) sts.

Row 1 (WS): Adjust the stitch count to 175 (199, 223, 253, 277, 301, 325, 349) sts by inc (or dec) evenly across the row. +1 (0, −2, +3, +1, 0, −2, −2) sts.

NOTE If you are modifying this garment, your st count must be a multiple of 6 + 7.

Row 2 (RS): K3, *p1, k5, rep from * to last 4 sts, p1, k3.

Row 3–9: Work sts as they appear (knit the knits, purl the purls).

The sts are divided into sets of knits (5 sts are in each set to start) and sets of purls (just 1 st to start in each set). On Inc rows, you will inc at beg and end of each set of knits and each set of purls to form the ribbed ruffle.

Row 10 (RS): K to last st in k group, m1, k1, *m1p, p1, m1p, k1, m1, k to last st in k group, m1, k1, rep from * to last p st, m1p, p1, m1p, k1, m1, k to end of row.

Rows 11–19: Work sts as they appear.

Row 20 (RS): K to last st in k group, m1, k1, *p1, m1p, p1, m1p, p1, k1, m1, k to last st in k group, m1, k1, rep from * to last p group, p1, m1p, p1, m1p, p1, k1, m1, k to end of row.

Rows 21–29: Work sts as they appear.

NOTE If you want a longer ruffle, you may add length here.

Row 30: BO in patt.

sleeves

You will work the sleeves in the round, using short rows to create the sleeve cap. At the same time, you will increase to form the ruffles. You can easily add length to the sleeve by working more rounds between inc rounds, but remember that more length will require more yarn.

With RS facing, use dpns to pick up and knit 60 (60, 66, 78, 78, 84, 90, 96) sts evenly around the armhole. (If you are modifying the garment, pick up a multiple of 6 sts.)

Join to work in the round, placing a st marker to indicate the end of round.

Round 1: K3, *p1, k5, rep from * to last 4 sts, p1, k3.

You will now work back and forth (short rows), shaping the sleeve cap and increasing for the ruffles. Read through the sections on sleeve-cap shaping and ruffle increases before continuing.

Shape Sleeve Cap

Work at the same time as ruffle increases. For w&t instructions, see the "Special Knitting Techniques" appendix.

Row 1: Work 40 (40, 44, 52, 52, 56, 60, 64) sts in patt, w&t.

Row 2: Work 20 (20, 22, 26, 26, 28, 30, 32) sts in patt, w&t.

Row 3: Work in patt to wrapped st, pick up wrap and work it together with the wrapped st, wrap next st and turn.

Rep Row 3 until 4 (4, 6, 10, 10, 12, 14, 14) sts total rem that have not been wrapped. 36 (36, 38, 42, 42, 44, 46, 50) rows have been worked for the sleeve.

RUFFLE INCREASES
(WORK AT THE SAME TIME AS CAP SHAPING)

NOTE Work increases only in groups of sts that are between the last 2 wraps.

*Inc row: Work to last st in a k or p group; m1 in patt; work the next st in patt; work 1 st; m1 in patt; *work to last st of group; m1 in patt; work 1 st; rep from * across ending with work 1 in patt; m1 in patt; work to 1 st beyond last wrap, picking up the wrap; w&t.*

Inc every 9 (9, 9, 10, 10, 11, 11, 12) rows 3 times.

Then work 9 (9, 11, 12, 12, 11, 13, 14) rows even.

The cap shaping is now complete. Continue working in the round.

Next round: Work to end of round, picking up wraps.

Next round: Work even, picking up remaining wraps.

Next round: Work Inc round, increasing at beg and end of every group of sts.

Work 2 rounds even.

You will now work short rows again to shape the edge of the sleeve. Add length over this section if desired.

Rows 1 and 2: Work to 18 sts before end of round, w&t.

Rows 3–8: Work to 1 st before wrapped st, w&t. A total of 8 sts have been wrapped.

Row 9: Work to marker, picking up wraps.

Continue in the round and work 1 round even, picking up rem wraps.

BO in patt.

crochet edging

NOTE See the "Special Knitting Techniques" appendix for instructions on single crochet (sc), double crochet (dc), and chain stitch.

Row 1: With crochet hook and RS of garment facing, begin at the hemline of the ruffle at one side and work 1 sc into every row and st up the front, around the neckline, and down the opposite front to the hemline of the ruffle. Chain 1 and turn.

Row 2: SC in every sc, working 3 sc in 1 sc at the 2 points where the neckline shaping begins and ends.

Row 3: SC to the point where neckline shaping begins, then work scalloped border along neckline as follows: *sc in next sc, skip 2 sc, 5dc in next sc, skip 2 sc, rep from * across entire neckline, easing the last few scallops if necessary to end with sc; sc in rem sc to end of row. Cut yarn and secure by pulling tail through last loop.

finishing

Weave in all ends. Block garment to desired measurement.

Sew one piece of the wider ribbon onto the right front at the point where neckline shaping started. Sew the second piece of the wider ribbon to the left side, even with the first ribbon.

Sew a 6" length of the thinner ribbon to beg of neckline shaping on the left front and to the WS of the garment on the RS. Depending on your body shape, you may want to add a second set of inside ribbons near the bottom ruffle.

Cut the raw edges of the ribbons at an angle to prevent fraying.

HOLLYHOCK
cap-sleeved top

by Jairlyn Mason

This cap-sleeved top, knit in a silk-merino blend, has stylish architecture and modern ornamentation like its namesake, Frank Lloyd Wright's Hollyhock House in Los Angeles, California, which was built for an independent woman with a passion for the arts. The scooped neck and subtle waist shaping make for a flattering silhouette that pairs equally well with a dressy skirt or your favorite jeans.

pattern notes

When directions are given for only some of the sizes (for example, "Sizes 1X and 2X Only"), and the size you are knitting is not listed, then continue the pattern at the "All Sizes" heading. An instruction that tells you to do something 0 times means this particular instruction does not apply to your size.

The charts used in this pattern are available for you to download and print at **www.wiley.com/go/knittinginthesun**.

directions
back

Using straight needles, CO 70 (80, 90, 100, 110, 120) sts.

Work 8 rows in k2, p2 rib, starting with k2.

Shape Waist

The remainder of the back is worked in St st.

Next row (RS): K1, k2tog, k to last 3 sts, ssk, k1.

Work 5 rows in St st.

Rep these 6 rows 3 (3, 3, 4, 4, 4) more times.
62 (72, 82, 90, 100, 110) sts.

Work 4 (8, 8, 8, 12, 14) rows in St st.

SIZE
XS (S, M, L, 1X, 2X)

FINISHED MEASUREMENTS
Chest circumference: 29 (33, 37, 40, 44, 48)"

Length: 20 (21, 21, 22, 23, 24)"

MATERIALS
- Malabrigo *Silky Merino* (50% silk, 50% baby merino wool; 150 yd. per 50g skein); color: 410 Spring Water; 4 (4, 5, 5, 6, 7) skeins
- US 6 (4mm) straight needles *(or size needed to match gauge)*
- US 6 (4mm) circular needle, 24" length
- Split-ring stitch markers
- Stitch holder or scrap yarn
- Tapestry needle

GAUGE
20 sts × 32 rows = 4" in St st

SKILLS USED
increasing, decreasing, following lace charts, picking up stitches

16-stitch Lacy Chain Chart

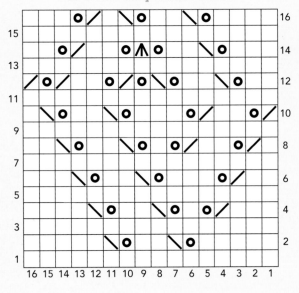

20-stitch Lacy Chain Chart

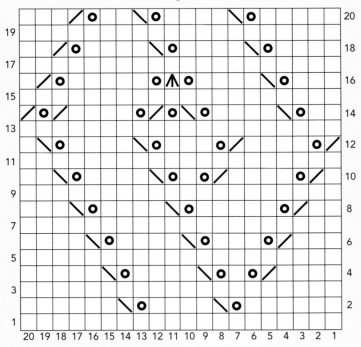

Key to Lacy Chain Charts

□	**knit** K on RS, P on WS	▱	**k2tog** Knit 2 sts together as 1 st	

ssk
 Slip 1 st as if to knit, slip another st as if to knit. Insert LH needle into front of these 2 sts and knit them together

⊙	**yo** yarn over	⋀	**s2kp** Slip 2 sts together as if to k2tog. Knit 1 st. Pass 2 slipped sts over the st just knit

Next row (RS): Kfb, k to last 2 sts, kfb, k1.

Work 7 rows in St st.

Rep these 8 rows 4 more times. 72 (82, 92, 100, 110, 120) sts.

Continue in St st until back measures 13 (13, 13, 14, 15, 16)" from the cast-on edge, ending with a WS row.

Shape Armholes

BO 4 (5, 5, 5, 5, 5) sts at beg of next 2 rows. 64 (72, 82, 90, 100, 110) sts.

Sizes 1X and 2X Only (other sizes continue below at "All Sizes")

BO 0 (0, 0, 0, 2, 3) sts at beg of next 2 rows. 64 (72, 82, 90, 96, 104) sts.

All Sizes

Next row (RS): K2, ssk, k to last 4 sts, k2tog, k2.

Next row (WS): Purl.

Rep last 2 rows 1 (3, 4, 4, 4, 6) more time(s). 60 (64, 72, 80, 86, 90) sts.

Continue in St st until armhole measures 5½ (6½, 6½, 6½, 6½, 6½)", ending with a WS row.

Divide for Neck

Next row (RS): K 20 (20, 20, 23, 23, 23), place these sts on holder (or scrap yarn) for right shoulder; BO 20 (24, 32, 34, 40, 44) sts; k to end.

Next row (WS): P 20 (20, 20, 23, 23, 23).

Left Shoulder

Next row (RS): BO 4 sts, k to end. 16 (16, 16, 19, 19, 19) sts.

Next row: Purl.

Next row: BO 3 sts, k to end.

Next row: Purl.

Rep last 2 rows once more. 10 (10, 10, 13, 13, 13) sts.

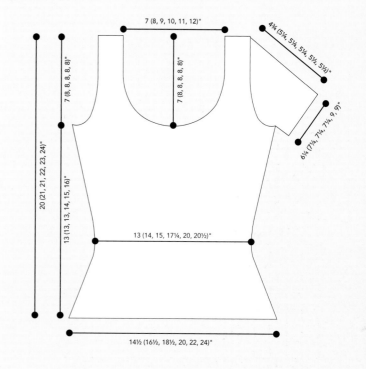

Continue in St st until armhole measures 7 (8, 8, 8, 8, 8)".

BO all sts.

Right Shoulder

Transfer sts from holder to needle. With RS facing, join a new ball of yarn at armhole edge.

Next row (RS): Knit.

Next row (WS): BO 4 sts, p to end. 16 (16, 16, 19, 19, 19) sts.

Next row: Knit.

Next row: BO 3 sts, p to end.

Next row: Knit.

Rep last 2 rows once more. 10 (10, 10, 13, 13, 13) sts.

Continue in St st until armhole measures 7 (8, 8, 8, 8, 8)".

BO all sts.

front

Using straight needles, CO 70 (80, 90, 100, 110, 120) sts.

All Sizes

Work 8 rows in k2, p2 ribbing, starting with k2.

Next row: K 27 (32, 37, 40, 45, 50), pm, k16 (16, 16, 20, 20, 20), pm, k to end of row.

Work as for Back including all shaping, but work Lacy Chain Pattern between markers, starting with Row 1 (a WS row), using the 16-stitch Lacy Chain Chart for sizes XS, S, and M and the 20-stitch Lacy Chain Chart for sizes L, 1X, and 2X.

Continue in patt as set until work measures 13 (13, 13, 14, 15, 16)" from cast-on edge, ending with a WS row. 72 (82, 92, 100, 110, 120) sts.

Shape Neck and Armholes

Next row (RS): BO 4 (5, 5, 5, 5, 5) sts; k 24 (28, 33, 35, 40, 45) sts to marker, then place these sts on holder for left shoulder; BO 16 (16, 16, 20, 20, 20) sts; k to end.

Next row (WS): BO 4 (5, 5, 5, 5, 5) sts, p to end.

Shape Right Armhole and Front Neck
Sizes L, 1X, and 2X Only

Next row (RS): K2, ssk, k to end.

Next row (WS): BO 0 (0, 0, 1, 2, 3) sts, p to last 4 sts, p2tog-tbl, p2. 24 (28, 33, 32, 36, 40) sts.

All Sizes

Next row (RS): K2, ssk, k to last 4 sts, k2tog, k2.

Next row (WS): P to last 4 sts, p2tog-tbl, p2.

Rep last 2 rows 1 (1, 1, 1, 2, 3) more time(s). 18 (22, 27, 26, 27, 28) sts.

Sizes S, M, L, 1X, and 2X Only

Next row (RS): K2, ssk, k to last 4 sts, k2tog, k2.

Next row (WS): Purl.

Rep last 2 rows 0 (1, 2, 1, 2, 0) more time(s). 18 (18, 21, 22, 21, 26) sts rem.

Size 2X Only

Next row (RS): K2, ssk, k to end.

Next row (WS): Purl.

Next row: K2, ssk, k to last 4 sts, k2tog, k2.

Next row: Purl.

Rep last 4 rows 1 more time. 18 (18, 21, 22, 21, 20) sts rem.

All Sizes

Next row (RS): K2, ssk, k to end.

Next row (WS): Purl.

Rep last 2 rows 3 (3, 6, 4, 5, 2) more times. 14 (14, 14, 17, 17, 17) sts.

Work 2 rows in St st.

Next row (RS): K2, ssk, k to end.

Work 3 rows in St st.

Rep last 4 rows 3 more times. 10 (10, 10, 13, 13, 13) sts.

Continue in St st until armhole measures 7 (8, 8, 8, 8, 8)".

BO all sts.

Shape Left Armhole and Front Neck

Transfer sts from holder to needle. With RS facing, join new yarn at armhole edge.

Sizes L, 1X, and 2X Only

Next row (RS): BO 0 (0, 0, 1, 2, 3) st(s), k to end.

Next row (WS): P2, p2tog, p to end.

All Sizes

Next row (RS): K2, ssk, k to last 4 sts, k2tog, k2.

Next row (WS): P2, p2tog, p to end.

Rep last 2 rows 1 (1, 1, 1, 2, 3) more time(s). 18 (22, 27, 26, 27, 28) sts.

Sizes S, M, L, 1X, and 2X Only

Next row (RS): K2, ssk, k to last 4 sts, k2tog, k2.

Next row (WS): Purl.

Rep last 2 rows 0 (1, 2, 1, 1, 0) more time(s). 18 (18, 21, 22, 23, 26) sts.

Size 2X Only

Next row (RS): K to last 4 sts, k2tog k2.

Next row (WS): Purl.

Next row: K2, ssk, k to last 4 sts, k2tog, k2.

Next row: Purl.

Rep last 4 rows 1 more time. 18 (18, 21, 22, 23, 20) sts.

All Sizes

Next row (RS): K to last 4 sts, k2tog k2.

Next row (WS): Purl.

Rep last 2 rows 3 (3, 6, 4, 5, 2) more times. 14 (14, 14, 17, 17, 17) sts.

Work 2 rows in St st.

Next row (RS): K to last 4 sts, k2tog k2.

Work 3 rows in St st.

Rep last 4 rows 3 more times. 10 (10, 10, 13, 13, 13) sts.

Continue in St st until armhole measures 7 (8, 8, 8, 8, 8)".

BO all sts.

sleeves

Using straight needles, CO 62 (72, 72, 72, 92, 92) sts.

Work 4 rows in k2, p2 rib, beg with k2.

Beg working in St st, starting with a knit row.

BO 4 (5, 5, 5, 5, 5) sts at beg of next 2 rows. 54 (62, 62, 62, 82, 82) sts.

BO 3 (3, 3, 3, 5, 5) sts at beg of next 2 rows. 48 (56, 56, 56, 72, 72) sts.

Next row (RS): K1, k2tog, k to last 3 sts, ssk, k1.

Next row (WS): Purl.

Rep last 2 rows 2 (2, 2, 2, 4, 4) more times. 42 (50, 50, 50, 62, 62) sts.

Work 2 rows in St st.

Next row (RS): K1, k2tog, k to last 3 sts, ssk, k1.

Work 3 rows in St st.

Rep last 4 rows 3 (4, 4, 4, 1, 1) more time(s). 34 (40, 40, 40, 58, 58) sts.

Next row (RS): K1, k2tog, k to last 3 sts, ssk, k1.

Next row (WS): Purl.

Rep last 2 rows 1 (0, 0, 0, 4, 4) more time(s). 30 (38, 38, 38, 48, 48) sts.

BO 3 sts at beg of next 4 (6, 6, 6, 8, 8) rows. 18 (20, 20, 20, 24, 24) sts.

BO rem sts.

finishing

Weave in ends. Block pieces to size. Sew shoulder seams.

neck band

Using circular needle and with RS facing, beg at right shoulder seam and pick up and knit 2 sts for every 3 rows to center back bind-off, pick up and knit 1 st in each st bound off for the back neck, pick up and knit 2 sts for every 3 rows up to left shoulder and down to center front, pick up and knit 1 st in each st bound off for front neck, pick up and knit 2 sts for every 3 rows to right shoulder. Place a marker to indicate beg of round.

The total number of sts picked up must be a multiple of 4. If necessary, dec in the first round to a multiple of 4 sts.

Work in k2, p2 rib for 3 rounds.

BO in patt.

Attach sleeves at armholes. Sew side seams.

TOFINO
top-down shaped t-shirt

by Sarah Sutherland

This easy tunic-length, scoop-necked tee is knit in the round from the top down. Clever rib detailing at the neck, waist, and hem accentuate its feminine lines, and it's perfect to wear on a trip to your favorite beach or as you navigate the city dreaming of some faraway locale.

directions

yoke

Using circular needle, CO 168 (192, 208, 232, 240) sts.

Join to work in the round, taking care not to twist the work, place marker (pm) to denote end of round.

Round 1: *K1, p1, rep from * to end of round.

Rep this round until yoke measures 1".

Next round: *K3, p1, rep from * to end of round.

Rep this round until yoke measures 2".

Next round: *K7, p1, rep from * to end of round.

Rep this round until yoke measure 3".

Next round: Knit.

Work in St st until yoke measures 4".

Next round: Inc 24 (24, 32, 32, 40) sts, using m1 increases, evenly spaced to 192 (216, 240, 264, 280) sts.

Continue working in St st until yoke measures 5".

Next round: Inc 24 (32, 32, 40, 48) sts evenly spaced to 216 (248, 272, 304, 328) sts.

Continue working in St st until yoke measures 6 (6, 6½, 6½, 6½)".

SIZE

S (M, L, 1X, 2X)

FINISHED MEASUREMENTS

Chest circumference: 32 (37, 41½, 45, 49½)"

Length: 25 (25, 25½, 25½, 26)"

MATERIALS

- Berroco *Bonsai* (97% bamboo, 3% nylon; 77 yd. per 50g skein); color: 4121 Raku Brown; 8 (9, 11, 12, 13) skeins
- US 5 (3.75mm) circular needle, 24" length (*or size needed to match gauge*)
- US 5 (3.75mm) double-pointed needles
- Stitch marker
- Tapestry needle
- Scrap yarn

GAUGE

20 sts × 32 rows = 4" in St st

SKILLS USED

knitting in the round, increasing, knitted cast-on

body

You will now divide the body and sleeves.

Next round: *Put next 44 (48, 48, 56, 56) sts on scrap yarn for sleeve, CO 16 sts using backward loop method or knitted cast-on, k 68 (76, 88, 96, 100), rep from * once. 160 (184, 208, 224, 248) sts.

Work even in St st until piece measures 9 (9, 9½, 9½, 10)".

Next round: *K7, p1, rep from * to end of round.

Rep this round until piece measures 11 (11, 11½, 11½, 12)".

Next round: *K3, p1, rep from * to end of round.

Rep this round until piece measures 13 (13, 13½, 13½, 14)".

Next round: *K1, p1, rep from * to end of round.

Rep this round until piece measures 15 (15, 15½, 15½, 16)".

Next round: *K3, p1, rep from * to end of round.

Rep this round until piece measures 17 (17, 17½, 17½, 18)".

Next round: *K7, p1, rep from * to end of round.

Rep this round until piece measures 19 (19, 19½, 19½, 20)".

Next round: Knit.

Continue working in St st until piece measures 20 (20, 20½, 20½, 21)".

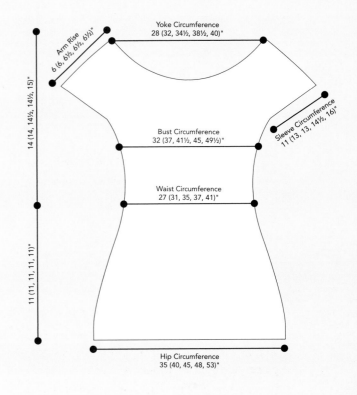

Next round: Inc 16 sts evenly spaced. 176 (200, 224, 240, 264) sts.

Continue working in St st until piece measures 24 (24, 24½, 24½, 25)".

Next round: *K1, p1, rep from * to end of round.

Rep this round until piece measures 25 (25, 25½, 25½, 26)".

BO in patt.

sleeves

Put the held stitches for one sleeve onto dpns; pick up and knit 12 (16, 16, 16, 24) sts from sts CO for the underarm. 56 (64, 64, 72, 80) sts.

Next round: *K1, p1, rep from * to end of round.

Rep this round for 1".

BO in patt.

Make the second sleeve the same.

finishing

Weave in ends. Block as desired.

BAY OF FUNDY
lace-detailed pullover
by Susan Robicheau

This top will take you through all seasons. It's got the ease and comfort of your favorite tee, but with plenty of style to take you anywhere. Simple finishes around the neck and sleeves keep it contemporary and unfussy; lace detailing up the front and on the sleeves add a feminine flourish. Knit in a pure soy yarn, it's got the look of your favorite wooly top, but with the cool feel of a plant fiber. For added wardrobe versatility, pair it with its companion cardigan, Bridgetown, on page 117.

pattern notes
bay of fundy lace pattern

(worked over 11 sts)

Row 1 and all WS rows: Purl.

Row 2 (RS): [Ssk] twice, [yo, k1] 3 times, yo, [k2tog] twice.

Row 4: Ssk, k3, yo, k1, yo, k3, k2tog.

Row 6: Ssk, k2, yo, k3, yo, k2, k2tog.

Row 8: Ssk, k1, yo, k5, yo, k1, k2tog.

Row 10: Ssk, yo, k1, yo, ssk, k1, k2tog, yo, k1, yo, k2tog.

Row 12: Ssk, yo, k2, yo, sk2p, yo, k2, yo, k2tog.

Row 14: K1, yo, k3, sk2p, k3, yo, k1.

Row 16: [K1, yo] twice, k2tog, sk2p, ssk, [yo, k1] twice.

Row 18: K1, yo, k3, sk2p, k3, yo, k1.

Row 20: K2, yo, k2, sk2p, k2, yo, k2.

Row 22: K3, yo, k1, sk2p, k1, yo, k3.

Row 24: K1, k2tog, yo, k1, yo, sk2p, yo, k1, yo, ssk, k1.

Row 26: Ssk, yo, k2, yo, sk2p, yo, k2, yo, k2tog.

Row 28: Ssk, k3, yo, k1, yo, k3, k2tog.

Rep rows 1–28 for patt.

SIZE
S (M, L, 1X, 2X, 3X)

FINISHED MEASUREMENTS
Chest circumference: 34 (38, 42, 46, 50, 54)"

Length: 20¾ (20¾, 22, 22, 23¼, 23¼)"

MATERIALS
- SWTC *Pure* (100% Soysilk, 150m per 50g ball); color: 81 Tuscany; 5 (7, 9, 10, 11, 12) skeins
- US 6 (4mm) straight needles *(or size needed to match gauge)*
- US 6 (4mm) circular needle, 16" length
- Stitch holders or scrap yarn
- Stitch markers
- Tapestry needle

GAUGE
21 sts × 26 rows = 4" in St st

SKILLS USED
increasing, decreasing, lace knitting, three-needle bind off, picking up stitches

directions

back

Using straight needles, CO 91 (101, 113, 123, 133, 143) sts.

Work 12 rows in St st, starting with a knit row.

Shape Waist

Next row (Dec row) (RS): K1, ssk, k to last 3 sts, k2tog, k1.

Continue in St st, and rep Dec row every 4th row twice more. 85 (95, 107, 117, 127, 137) sts.

Work 5 rows even.

Next row (Inc row) (RS): K1, m1, k to last st, m1, k1.

Rep Inc row every 4th row twice more. 91 (101, 113, 123, 133, 143) sts.

Continue to work even in St st until back measures 13½" (all sizes), ending with a WS row.

Shape Armholes

BO 4 (5, 6, 6, 7, 7) sts at beg of next 2 rows.

Next row (RS): K2, ssk, k to last 4 sts, k2tog, k2.

Next row: Purl.

Rep last 2 rows 2 (2, 6, 8, 8, 9) more times. 77 (85, 87, 93, 101, 111) sts.

Continue to work even in St st until 30 (36, 40, 46, 48, 52) rows are complete from beg of armhole shaping.

Shape Back Neck

Next row (RS): K26 (28, 28, 30, 32, 35), place next 25 (29, 31, 33, 37, 41) sts on holder, k1, ssk, k to end of row. Continue on this side of neck only.

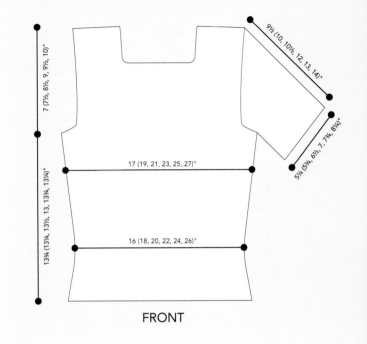

17 (19, 21, 23, 25, 27)"

16 (18, 20, 22, 24, 26)"

7 (7½, 8½, 9, 9½, 10)"

13¾ (13¾, 13½, 13, 13¾, 13¾)"

9½ (10, 10½, 12, 13, 14)"

5¼ (5¾, 6½, 7, 7¾, 8½)"

FRONT

Next row: Purl.

Row 1: K1, ssk, k to end of row.

Row 2: Purl.

Rep last 2 rows 3 (3, 3, 4, 5, 5) more times. 21 (23, 23, 24, 25, 28) sts. Transfer these sts to holder. Break yarn.

Attach yarn to opposite side of neck, with RS facing.

Row 1: K to last 3 sts, k2tog, k1.

Row 2: Purl.

Rep last 2 rows 4 (4, 4, 5, 6, 6) more times. 21 (23, 23, 24, 25, 28) sts. Transfer these sts to holder. Break yarn.

front

Using straight needles, CO 91 (101, 113, 123, 133, 143) sts.

Row 1 and all WS rows: Purl.

Row 2: K40 (45, 51, 56, 61, 66), pm, begin working Bay of Fundy Lace Pattern over 11 sts starting with Row 2, pm, k40 (45, 51, 56, 61, 66).

Continue working Bay of Fundy Lace Pattern over center 11 sts while shaping the waist at the same time.

Shape Waist

Rows 12, 16 and 20: K1, ssk, work in patt to last 3 sts, k2tog, k1.

Rows 26, 30, and 34 (Rows 30 and 34 correspond to Rows 2 and 6 of the next rep of the lace panel): K1, m1, work in patt to last st, m1, k1.

Continue to work in patt until front measures the same as back to beg of armhole shaping.

Shape Armholes

Continue in patt and BO 4 (5, 6, 6, 7, 7) sts at beg of next 2 rows.

Next row: K2, ssk, k to last 4 sts, k2tog, k2.

Next row: Purl.

Rep last 2 rows 2 (2, 6, 8, 8, 9) more times. 77 (85, 87, 93, 101, 111) sts.

Continue to work even, maintaining the Bay of Fundy Lace Pattern until 22 (26, 24, 28, 22, 26) rows are complete from beg of armhole shaping, ending with row 28 of the Bay of Fundy Lace Pattern.

Shape Neck

Next row: K26 (28, 28, 30, 32, 35), place next 25 (29, 31, 33, 37, 41) sts on holder, k1, ssk, k to end of row. Continue working this side of neck only.

Next row: Purl.

Next row (Dec row): K1, ssk, k to end of row.

Rep Dec row every RS row 3 (3, 3, 4, 5, 5) more times. 21 (23, 23, 24, 25, 28) sts.

Work even in St st until 46 (50, 56, 60, 62, 66) rows are complete from beg of armhole shaping. Transfer these sts to holder. Break yarn.

Attach yarn to rem 26 (28, 28, 30, 32, 35) sts with RS facing.

Next row: K to last 3 sts, k2tog, k1.

Next row: Purl.

Rep last 2 rows 4 (4, 4, 5, 6, 6) more times. 21 (23, 23, 24, 25, 28) sts.

Work even in St st until 46 (50, 56, 60, 62, 66) rows are complete from beg of armhole shaping. Transfer sts to holder. Break yarn.

sleeves

(make 2)

Using straight needles, CO 55 (61, 69, 75, 81, 87) sts.

Row 1 and all WS rows: P19 (22, 26, 29, 32, 35), pm, k1, p15, k1, pm, p19 (22, 26, 29, 32, 35).

Row 2: K to marker, sm, p1, k1, [k2tog] twice, [yo, k1] 3 times, yo, [ssk] twice, k3, p1, sm, k to end of row.

Row 4: K to marker, sm, p1, [k2tog] twice, yo, k1, yo, k3, yo, k1, yo, [ssk] twice, k2, p1, sm, k to end of row.

Row 6: K to marker, sm, p1, k3, [k2tog] twice, [yo, k1] 3 times, yo, [ssk] twice, k1, p1, sm, k to end of row.

Row 8: K to marker, sm, p1, k2, [k2tog] twice, yo, k1, yo, k3, yo, k1, yo, [ssk] twice, p1, sm, k to end of row.

Rep Rows 1–8 once more.

Work remainder of sleeve in St st.

Row 1: K1, m1, k to last st, m1, k1.

Rows 2–4: Work in St st.

Rep these 4 rows 3 (3, 3, 4, 4, 5) times. 63 (69, 77, 85, 91, 99) sts.

Continue to work even until 18 (18, 18, 24, 24, 28) St st rows are complete. Sleeve measures 4 (4, 4, 5, 5, 5½)".

BO 4 (5, 6, 6, 7, 7) sts at beg of next 2 rows.

Next row: K1, ssk, k to last 3 sts, k2tog, k1.

Next row: Purl.

Rep last 2 rows until 19 (19, 21, 25, 25, 29) sts rem.

BO all sts.

collar

Use three-needle bind-off (see "Special Knitting Techniques" appendix) to join front and back at shoulders.

Using 16" circular needle, with RS facing, join yarn at right shoulder, k 25 (29, 31, 33, 37, 41) sts from holder at back neck, pick up and knit 9 (9, 9, 10, 12, 12) sts from left back neck edge and 19 (19, 24, 25, 32, 32) sts along left front neck edge, k 25 (29, 31, 33, 37, 41) sts from stitch holder at front neck, pick up and knit 19 (19, 24, 25, 32, 32) sts along right front edge and 9 (9, 9, 10, 12, 12) sts along right back edge. 106 (114, 128, 136, 160, 168) sts.

Work 6 rounds in garter st (knit a round, purl a round) starting with a knit round.

BO.

finishing

Sew side seams and sleeve seams. Sew sleeves into armholes. Weave in ends. Block with steam, or according to your own preference.

LONG SLEEVES

PUGET SOUND
drop-stitch sweater
by Kristi Porter

This pullover gives you the comfort of a favorite sweatshirt with loads more style. The top, worked up in a cottony-feeling silk-wool blend, gives you coolness and plenty of coverage—perfect protection from the sun or the office air conditioner. The elongated stitches over the lower arms and torso allow a bit of light and plenty of air to pass through. The empire waist and rounded neckline are easy to wear and flattering to many body types. You might even want to knit more than one!

pattern notes
elongated stockinette stitch

Row 1 (RS): *Insert needle into next st and k, wrapping yarn twice around right needle, rep from * across.

Row 2 (WS): Purl, allowing extra wraps to fall.

Rep these 2 rows for Elongated Stockinette Stitch.

directions
back

CO 88 (98, 108, 120, 130, 140) sts using larger needles.

Switch to size 7 needles (or those needed to match gauge) and purl 1 row.

Work Elongated Stockinette Stitch for a total of 40 rows. Piece will measure approximately 10", but will measure 13" when blocked.

Switch to St st and work even until the St st portion measures 4 (4, 4, 4, 4½, 4½)", ending with a WS row.

SIZE
S (M, L, 1X, 2X, 3X)

FINISHED MEASUREMENTS
Chest circumference: 35 (39, 43, 48, 52, 56)"

Length: 26½ (26½, 27, 27, 28, 28)"

MATERIALS
- Cascade Yarns *Venezia Worsted* (70% merino wool, 30% silk; 219 yd. per 100g skein); color: 124; 5 (6, 6, 7, 7, 8) skeins
- Size 7 (4.5 mm) needles *(or size needed to match gauge)*
- Size 9 (5.5 mm) needles *(or 2 sizes larger than those needed to match gauge)*
- Size 6 (4 mm) circular needle, 16" length
- Stitch holder
- Stitch markers or safety pins
- Tapestry needle

continued ➤

continued ➤

GAUGE

20 sts × 26 rows = 4" in St st

14 sts × 12 rows = 4" over Elongated Stockinette Stitch, blocked

14 sts × 16 rows = 4" over Elongated Stockinette Stitch, unblocked

SKILLS USED

decreasing, increasing, picking up stitches

Shape Armholes

BO 4 (4, 6, 8, 10, 13) sts at beg of next 2 rows.

BO 2 (2, 3, 3, 5, 5) sts at beg of next 2 rows.

Next (Dec) row (RS): K2, ssk, k to last 4 sts, k2tog, k2.

Next row: Purl.

Rep these 2 rows 0 (1, 1, 6, 4, 7) more time(s). 74 (82, 86, 86, 90, 90) sts rem.

Shape Neck

Work even until Back measures 6" from beg of armhole, ending with a WS row, then shape neck and shoulders.

K27 (31, 32, 32, 35, 35), place these sts on a holder or spare needle, join a second ball of yarn and BO center 20 sts, k to end of row.

Left Neck and Shoulder

Row 1 (WS): Purl.

Row 2 (RS): K2, ssk, k to end.

Rep these 2 rows 5 (6, 4, 4, 4, 4) more times. 21 (24, 27, 27, 30, 30) sts.

Work even in St st until piece measures 8½ (8½, 9, 9, 9½, 9½)" from beg of armhole shaping, ending with a RS row.

BO 7 (8, 9, 9, 10, 10) sts at beg of next 3 WS rows.

Right Neck and Shoulder

Transfer sts held for right shoulder onto needle.

Row 1 (WS): Purl.

Row 2 (RS): K to last 4 sts, k2tog, k2.

Rep these 2 rows 5 (6, 4, 4, 4, 4) more times. 21 (24, 27, 27, 30, 30) sts.

Work even in St st until piece measures 8½ (8½, 9, 9, 9½, 9½)" from beg of armhole shaping, ending with a WS row.

BO 7 (8, 9, 9, 10, 10) sts at beg of next 3 RS rows.

front

Work same as Back through the armhole shaping and until the Front measures 3" from beg of armhole, ending with a WS row, then shape neck and shoulders.

Divide for Neck

K27 (31, 32, 32, 35, 35), then place these sts on a holder, join a second ball of yarn and BO center 20 sts, k to end of row.

Right Neck and Shoulder

Row 1 (WS): Purl.

Row 2 (RS): K2, ssk, k to end.

Rep these 2 rows 5 (6, 4, 4, 4, 4) more times. 21 (24, 27, 27, 30, 30) sts.

Work even in St st until piece measures 8½ (8½, 9, 9, 9½, 9½)" from beg of armhole shaping, ending with a RS row.

BO 7 (8, 9, 9, 10, 10) sts at beg of next 3 WS rows.

Left Neck and Shoulder

Transfer sts held for right shoulder onto needle.

Row 1 (WS: Purl.

Row 2 (RS): K to last 4 sts, k2tog, k2.

Rep these 2 rows 5 (6, 4, 4, 4, 4) more times. 21 (24, 27, 27, 30, 30) sts.

Work even in St st until piece measures 8½ (8½, 9, 9, 9½, 9½)" from beg of armhole shaping, ending with a WS row.

BO 7 (8, 9, 9, 10, 10) sts at beg of next 3 RS rows.

sleeves

(make 2)

Using larger needle, CO 50 (52, 56, 56, 60, 66) sts.

Switch to size 7 needles and work in Elongated Stockinette Stitch for 24 rows. Piece will measure about 6", but will measure 8" when blocked.

Switch to St st and inc 1 st at each end of needle every 4th row 0 (0, 6, 13, 15, 15) times, then every 6th row 8 (9, 5, 0, 0, 0) times. *Work Inc rows as follows:* K1, m1, k to last st, m1, k1. 66 (70, 78, 82, 90, 96) sts.

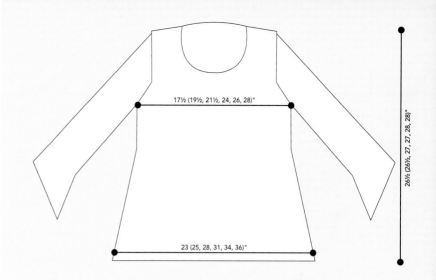

Work even until St st portion of sleeve measures 9 (9, 9, 10, 10, 10)", ending with a WS row.

BO 4 (4, 6, 8, 10, 13) sts at beg of next 2 rows.

BO 2 (2, 3, 3, 5, 5) sts at beg of next 2 rows.

Next row (Dec Row): K2, ssk, k to last 4 sts, k2tog, k2.

Next row: Purl.

Rep these 2 rows 16 (20, 21, 21, 21, 21) more times.

BO rem 16 sts.

finishing

Block pieces to measurements given.

Sew shoulder seams. Sew sleeves into armhole openings. Sew side and sleeve seams.

Place markers or safety pins every 2" around the neckline. Using size 6 circular needle, pick up and knit 9 sts between each set of markers, or about 4½ sts per inch. Join the work in the round. Work in garter st (purl 1 round, knit 1 round) for 1". BO all sts.

Weave in ends.

ALISHAN
hooded pullover

ALISHAN
hooded pullover

by Anne Kuo Lukito

This lightweight hooded pullover is carefully crafted for warmer climates. Using a yarn that's a blend of cool linen and warm mohair, loose stitches still have plenty of structure while allowing the cool breeze to blow through. The design cleverly uses the yarn doubled over panels on the center front and back keeping your core warm and creating a slimming silhouette. When night falls, the hood adds even more warmth.

pattern notes

You will work the center front and center back of the garment with two strands of yarn held together, but you will use a single strand for the rest of the garment. When working double stranded, work from a second ball of yarn or a bobbin. When working the shoulders on the front of the sweater, you need to use a smaller third bobbin. Unless indicated, work with one strand of yarn.

Since this pattern features open stitches, subtle increases make a difference. This pattern uses a **lifted increase** worked as follows: Working on the knit side, pull the LH needle toward you and down so that the back of the work is visible. Insert the tip of the RH needle, from the top down, into the top of the stitch in the row below the stitch on the needle. Knit this stitch, then knit the stitch on the LH needle.

In the pattern, the double-stranded sections are marked with bold text.

directions
front
Garter-Stitch Border
CO 61 (69, 77, 85, 93) sts using longer circular needle.

SIZE
XS (S, M, L, 1X)

FINISHED MEASUREMENTS
Chest circumference: 34 (38, 42, 46, 50)"

Length: 23 (23½, 24, 25½, 26)"

MATERIALS
- Louet *KidLin* (49% linen, 35% kid mohair, 16% nylon; 250 yd. per 50g skein); color: 59 Regimental Red; 5 (6, 6, 7, 8) skeins
- US 7 (4.5mm) circular needle, 24" or longer (*or size needed to match gauge*)
- US 7 (4.5mm) circular needle, 16" or longer
- US 7 (4.5mm) double-pointed needles
- Stitch markers
- Stitch holders or scrap yarn
- Tapestry needle
- Yarn bobbins, optional

continued ➤

continued ➤

GAUGE

16 sts × 21 rows = 4" in St st, single-stranded, after blocking

SKILLS USED

increasing, decreasing, Kitchener stitch (grafting), working with more than 1 strand of yarn at a time

Row 1 (WS): K20 (20, 24, 24, 28), place marker (pm), add a second strand of yarn and **k21 (29, 29, 37, 37),** pm, drop the second strand and k single stranded to end of row.

Rows 2 and 3: Knit, double-stranding between markers.

Body

Row 1 (RS): K1, [k3, p1] 4 (4, 5, 5, 6) times, k3, **k with 2 strands between markers,** k3, [p1, k3] 4 (4, 5, 5, 6) times, k1.

Row 2: Purl to marker, **p with 2 strands between markers,** p to end.

Rep these 2 rows until piece measures 3½ (3½, 4, 4, 4½)" from the cast-on edge.

Set Up Kangaroo Pocket

You will now double the number of sts over the center section where the pocket will form. You will slip half of these sts to a holder and later pick them up to create the pocket. You will continue knitting the body on the rem sts. Continue to use the yarn doubled over in this section. Remember that bold text indicates sts that are worked with the yarn held double.

Next row (RS): K1, [k3, p1] 4 (4, 5, 5, 6) times, k3, slip marker (sm), **k1 (4, 4, 7, 7), kfb 19 (21, 21, 23, 23) times, k1 (4, 4, 7, 7),** sm, k3, [p1, k3] 4 (4, 5, 5, 6) times, k1.

Next row: P to marker, **p2 (5, 5, 8, 8), *sl next st to st holder or spare needle held to the RS (the back) of the work, p1 with working needle, rep from * until 19 (21, 21, 23, 23) sts are on holder, p1 (4, 4, 7, 7),** sm, p to end. 61 (69, 77, 85, 93) sts on the needle.

Continue rep Rows 1 and 2 for 5". The front measures 8½ (8½, 9, 9, 9½)".

Create Kangaroo Pocket

Transfer the 19 (21, 21, 23, 23) pocket sts to a second needle. Work the pocket double stranded.

Starting on the WS of the pocket, CO 1 st using the backward loop method, p to end, CO 1 st using the backward loop. 21 (23, 23, 25, 25) sts.

Work in St st for 6 more rows, starting with a knit row, then shape the pocket.

Row 1 (RS): Ssk, k to last 2 sts, k2tog. 19 (21, 21, 23, 23) sts.

Rows 2, 4, and 6: K3, p to last 3 sts, k3.

Rows 3 and 5: Knit.

Row 7: K2, ssk, k to last 4 sts, k2tog, k2.

Rep Rows 2–7 of pocket shaping twice more. 13 (15, 15, 17, 17) sts.

Rep Rows 1–5 of pocket shaping once.

Leave sts on the needle.

Join Pocket to Body
Resume working on the body.

Next row: K1, [k3, p1] 4 (4, 5, 5, 6) times, k3, sm, **k4 (7, 7, 10, 10), hold the pocket sts parallel to the body sts, *put the needle through the first st of the pocket and the next st on body and knit these 2 sts tog; rep from * until the pocket is attached, k4 (7, 7, 10, 10),** sm, k3, [p1, k3] 4 (4, 5, 5, 6) times, k1.

Next row: Purl.

Rep Rows 1 and 2 of Body until piece measures 9¾ (9¾, 10¼, 10¾, 10¾)" from cast-on edge.

Shape Center Panel
You will now shape the center panel by working fewer sts double stranded. The overall st count does not change.

Row 1 (RS): Work in patt to marker, remove marker, k1 single stranded, replace marker, work double stranded to 1 st before marker, pm, k1 single stranded, remove marker, work to end of row in patt.

Rows 2–6: Work in patt, double stranding between markers.

Rep these 6 rows 3 more times. 13 (21, 21, 29, 29) sts between markers.

Work 2 rows even in patt.

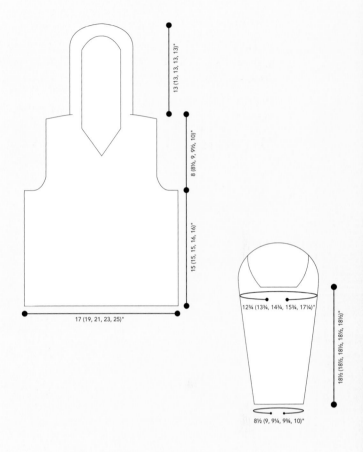

Shape Armholes and Neck
Row 1: BO 4 (4, 5, 5, 5) sts, k0 (0, 3, 3, 3), [p1, k3] 5 (5, 5, 5, 6) times, sm, **k13 (21, 21, 29, 29),** sm, [k3, p1] 6 (6, 7, 7, 8) times.

Row 2: BO 4 (4, 5, 5, 5) sts, p to end. 53 (61, 67, 75, 83) sts.

Row 3: BO 2 (2, 3, 3, 3) sts, k2 (2, 0, 0, 0), [p1, k3] 3 (3, 4, 4, 5) times, p1, k2, pm, **k1, remove marker, k13 (21, 21, 29, 29), remove marker, k1,** pm, k2, [p1, k3] 4 (4, 5, 5, 6) times, p1 (1, 0, 0, 0).

Row 4: BO 2 (2, 3, 3, 3) sts, p to end. 49 (57, 61, 69, 77) sts.

Row 5: BO 2 sts, k13 (14, 15, 16, 20), pm, **k2 (1, 2, 1, 1), remove marker, k15 (23, 23, 31, 31), remove marker, k2 (1, 2, 1, 1),** pm, k15 (16, 17, 18, 22).

Row 6: BO 2 sts, p to end, removing last marker as you work across row. 45 (53, 57, 65, 73) sts; 19 (25, 27, 33, 33) sts between markers.

NOTE After row 6, the double-stranded work forks for the neckline and shoulders. You'll need to use a 3rd small bobbin on yarn in order for this to work.

Size M Only: Work 2 Additional Rows As Follows:

Extra Row 1: K13, **k13,** k5, **k13,** k13.

Extra Row 2: Work sts as they appear.

Size L Only: Work 4 Additional Rows As Follows:

Extra Row 1: BO 1, k14, **k35,** k15.

Extra Row 2: BO 1, work sts as they appear.

Extra Row 3: K13, **k16,** k5, **k16,** k13.

Extra Row 4: Work sts as they appear.

Size 1X only: Work 4 Additional Rows As Follows:

Extra Row 1: BO 1, k18, **k35,** k19.

Extra Row 2: BO 1, work sts as they appear.

Extra Row 3: BO 1, k16, **k16,** k5, **k16,** k17.

Extra Row 4: BO 1, work sts as they appear.

All Sizes Continue:

Row 7: K11 (12, 11, 12, 14), **k10 (12, 14, 16, 16),** k3 (5, 7, 7, 9), **k10 (12, 14, 16, 16),** k11 (12, 11, 12, 14).

Rows 8 and 10: Work sts as they appear.

Row 9: K10 (11, 10, 11, 13), **k9 (12, 13, 15, 15),** k7 (7, 11, 11, 13), **k9 (12, 13, 15, 15),** k10 (11, 10, 11, 13).

Row 11: K9 (10, 9, 10, 12), **k8 (11, 12, 14, 14),** k5, BO 1 (1, 5, 5, 7) st(s), k5, **k8 (11, 12, 14, 14),** k9 (10, 9, 10, 12).

Right Shoulder

Slip the first stitch purlwise at the beginning of odd-numbered rows.

Row 12: P9 (10, 9, 10, 12), **p8 (11, 12, 14, 14),** p5, put rest of sts on holder.

Row 13: Sl 1, ssk, k3 (4, 4, 4, 4), **k8 (10, 10, 13, 13),** k8 (9, 9, 9, 11).

Row 14 and all even rows: P across row, working sts as they appear.

Row 15: Sl 1, ssk, k3 (4, 4, 4, 4) **k7 (9, 10, 12, 13),** k8 (9, 8, 9, 10).

Row 17: Sl 1, ssk, k3 (4, 4, 4, 4) **k7 (9, 9, 12, 12),** k7 (8, 8, 8, 10).

Row 19: Sl 1, ssk, k3 (4, 4, 4, 4) **k6 (8, 9, 11, 12),** k7 (8, 7, 8, 9).

Row 21: Sl 1, ssk, k3 (4, 4, 4, 4) **k6 (8, 8, 11, 11),** k6 (7, 7, 7, 9).

Row 23: Sl 1, ssk, k3 (4, 4, 4, 4) **k5 (7, 8, 10, 11),** k6 (7, 6, 7, 8).

Row 25: Sl 1, ssk, k3 (3, 3, 4, 4) **k5 (8, 8, 10, 10),** k5 (6, 6, 6, 8).

Row 27: Sl 1, ssk, k2 (3, 3, 4, 4) **k5 (7, 8, 9, 10),** k5 (6, 5, 6, 7).

Row 29: Sl 1, ssk, k1 (3, 3, 4, 4) **k5 (7, 7, 8, 9),** k5 (5, 5, 6, 7).

Row 31: Sl 1, ssk, k0 (3, 3, 4, 4) **k5 (6, 6, 7, 9),** k5 (5, 5, 6, 6).

Row 33: Sl 1, ssk 0 (1, 1, 1, 1) time(s), k3 (3, 3, 4, 4) **k5 (5, 5, 6, 8),** k5 (5, 5, 6, 6).

Row 35: Sl 1, ssk 0 (1, 0, 1, 1) time(s), k3 (2, 3, 4, 4), **k5 (5, 5, 5, 7),** k5 (5, 5, 6, 6). 14 (14, 15, 17, 19) sts.

Size XS Only:

End with Row 36. Continue with shoulder shaping.

Sizes S, M, L, and 1X:

Row 37: Sl 1, ssk – (0, 1, 1, 1) time(s), k– (3, 2, 3, 4), **k– (5, 5, 5, 6),** k– (5, 5, 6, 6).

Row 39: Sl 1, ssk – (0, 0, 0, 1) time(s), k– (3, 3, 4, 3), **k– (5, 5, 5, 6),** k– (5, 5, 6, 6).

Size S Only:

End with Row 40. Continue with shoulder shaping.

Sizes M, L, and 1X:

Row 41: Sl 1, k– (–, 3, 4, 4), **k– (– 5, 5, 6),** k– (–, 5, 6, 6), 14 (14, 14, 16, 17) sts.

Size M Only:

End with Row 42. Continue with shoulder shaping.

Sizes L and 1X:

Row 43: Sl 1, k– (–, –, 4, 4), **k– (–, –, 5, 6),** k– (–, –, 6, 6).

Size L Only:

End with Row 44. Continue with shoulder shaping.

Size 1X Only:

Rep Rows 43 and 44 two more times.

End with Row 48.

All sizes continue with shoulder shaping.

Shape Shoulder

There are 14 (14, 14, 16, 17) sts.

Next row (RS): Work in patt.

Next row (WS): BO 4 (4, 4, 5, 5) sts at armhole edge, work to end in patt.

Rep these 2 rows once more.

BO rem sts.

Left Shoulder

Transfer sts from holder to working needles.

Slip the first st purlwise at the beg of even-numbered rows.

Row 12 (WS): Sl 1, p4, **p8 (11, 12, 14, 14),** p9 (10, 9, 10, 12).

Row 13: K8 (9, 9, 9, 11), **k8 (10, 10, 13, 13),** k3 (4, 4, 4, 4), k2tog, k1.

Row 14 and all even rows: Sl 1, p across row, working sts as they appear.

Row 15: K8 (9, 8, 9, 10), **k7 (9, 10, 12, 13),** k3 (4, 4, 4, 4), k2tog, k1.

Row 17: K7 (8, 8, 8, 10), **k7 (9, 9, 12, 12),** k3 (4, 4, 4, 4), k2tog, k1.

Row 19: K7 (8, 7, 8, 9), **k6 (8, 9, 11, 12),** k3 (4, 4, 4, 4), k2tog, k1.

Row 21: K6 (7, 7, 7, 9), **k6 (8, 8, 11, 11),** k3 (4, 4, 4, 4), k2tog, k1.

Row 23: K6 (7, 6, 7, 8), **k5 (7, 8, 10, 11),** k3 (4, 4, 4, 4), k2tog, k1.

Row 25: K5 (6, 6, 6, 8), **k6 (8, 8, 10, 10),** k3 (3, 3, 4, 4), k2tog, k1.

Row 27: K5 (6, 5, 6, 7), **k5 (7, 8, 9, 10),** k3 (3, 3, 4, 4), k2tog, k1.

Row 29: K5 (5, 5, 6, 7), **k5 (7, 7, 8, 9),** k3 (3, 3, 4, 4), k2tog, k1.

Row 31: K5 (5, 5, 6, 6), **k5 (6, 6, 7, 9),** k2 (3, 3, 4, 4), k2tog, k1.

Row 33: K5 (5, 5, 6, 6), **k5 (5, 5, 6, 8),** k3 (3, 3, 4, 4), k2tog 0 (1, 1, 1, 1) time(s), k1.

Row 35: K5 (5, 5, 6, 6), **k5 (5, 5, 5, 7)**, k3 (2, 5, 4, 4), k2tog 0 (1, 0, 1, 1) time(s), k1.

Size XS Only:

End with Row 36. Continue with shoulder shaping.

Sizes S, M, L, and 1X:

Row 37: K– (5, 5, 6, 6), **k– (5, 5, 5, 6)**, k– (3, 2, 3, 4), k2tog – (0, 1, 1, 1) time(s), k1.

Row 39: K– (5, 5, 6, 6), **k– (5, 5, 5, 6)**, k– (3, 3, 4, 3), k2tog – (0, 0, 0, 1) time(s), k1.

Size S Only:

End with Row 40. Continue with shoulder shaping.

Sizes M, L, and 1X:

Row 41: K– (–, 5, 6, 6), **k– (–, 5, 5, 6)**, k– (–, 4, 5, 5).

Size M Only:

End with Row 42. Continue with shoulder shaping.

Sizes L and 1X:

Row 43: K– (–, –, 6, 6), **k– (–, –, 5, 6)**, k– (–, –, 5, 5).

Size L Only:

End with Row 44. Continue with shoulder shaping.

Size 1X Only:

Rep Rows 43 and 44 two more times.

End with Row 48.

All sizes continue with shoulder shaping.

Shape Shoulder

There are 14 (14, 14, 16, 17) sts.

Next row (RS): BO 4 (4, 4, 5, 5) sts at armhole edge, continue in patt to end of row.

Next row (WS): Work in patt.

Rep these 2 rows once more.

BO rem sts.

back

Body

Work Rows 1 and 2 of Front Body until piece measures 9¾ (9¾, 10¼, 10¾, 10¾)" from cast-on edge.

Shape Center Panel

Work as for Front.

Shape Armholes and Neck

Work as for Front through Row 10.

Row 11: K9 (10, 9, 10, 12), **k8 (11, 12, 14, 14)**, k11 (11, 15, 15, 17), **k8 (11, 12, 14, 14)**, k9 (10, 9, 10, 12).

Row 12 and all even rows: Work sts as they appear.

Row 13: K8 (9, 9, 9, 11), **k8 (10, 10, 13, 13)**, k13 (15, 15, 19, 21), **k8 (10, 10, 13, 13)**, k8 (9, 9, 9, 11).

Row 15: K8 (9, 8, 9, 10), **k7 (9, 10, 12, 13)**, k15 (17, 17, 21, 23), **k7 (9, 10, 12, 13)**, k8 (9, 8, 9, 10).

Row 17: K7 (8, 8, 8, 10), **k7 (9, 9, 12, 12)**, k17 (19, 19, 23, 25), **k7 (9, 9, 12, 12)**, k7 (8, 8, 8, 10).

Row 19: K7 (8, 7, 8, 9), **k6 (8, 9, 11, 12)**, k19 (21, 21, 25, 27), **k6 (8, 9, 11, 12)**, k7 (8, 7, 8, 9).

Row 21: K6 (7, 7, 7, 9), **k6 (8, 8, 11, 11)**, k21 (23, 23, 27, 29), **k6 (8, 8, 11, 11)**, k6 (7, 7, 7, 9).

Row 23: K6 (7, 6, 7, 8), **k5 (7, 8, 10, 11)**, k23 (25, 29, 29, 31), **k5 (7, 8, 10, 11)**, k6 (7, 6, 7, 8).

Row 25: K5 (6, 6, 6, 8), **k6 (8, 8, 10, 10)**, k23 (25, 29, 31, 33), **k6 (8, 8, 10, 10)**, k5 (6, 6, 6, 8).

Row 27: K5 (6, 5, 6, 7), **k5 (7, 8, 9, 10)**, k25 (27, 31, 33, 35), **k5 (7, 8, 9, 10)**, k5 (6, 5, 6, 7).

Row 29: K5 (5, 5, 6, 7), **k5 (7, 7, 8, 9),** k25 (29, 33, 35, 37), **k5 (7, 7, 8, 9),** k5 (5, 5, 6, 7).

Row 31: K5 (5, 5, 6, 6), **k5 (6, 6, 7, 9),** k25 (31, 35, 37, 39), **k5 (6, 6, 7, 9),** k5 (5, 5, 6, 6).

Row 33: K5 (5, 5, 6, 6), **k5 (5, 5, 6, 8),** k25 (33, 37, 39, 41), **k5 (5, 5, 6, 8),** k5 (5, 5, 6, 6).

Row 35: K5 (5, 5, 6, 6), **k5 (5, 5, 5, 7),** k25 (33, 37, 41, 43), **k5 (5, 5, 5, 7),** k5 (5, 5, 6, 6).

Size XS Only:

End with Row 36. Continue with shoulder shaping.

Sizes S, M, L, and 1X:

Row 37: K– (5, 5, 6, 6), **k– (5, 5, 5, 6),** k– (33, 37, 41, 45), **k– (5, 5, 5, 6),** k– (5, 5, 6, 6).

Rows 39: Rep Row 37.

Size S Only:

End with Row 40. Continue with shoulder shaping.

Sizes M, L, and 1X:

Row 41: K– (–, 5, 6, 6), **k– (–, 5, 5, 6),** k– (–, 37, 41, 45), **k– (–, 5, 5, 6),** k– (–, 5, 6, 6).

Size M Only:

End with Row 42. Continue with shoulder shaping.

Sizes L and 1X:

Row 43: K– (–, –, 6, 6), **k– (–, –, 5, 6),** k– (–, –, 41, 45), **k– (–, –, 5, 6),** k– (–, –, 6, 6).

Size L Only:

End with Row 44. Continue with shoulder shaping.

Size 1X Only:

Rep Rows 43 and 44 twice more. End with Row 48.

All sizes continue with shoulder shaping.

Shape Shoulders

BO 4 (4, 4, 5, 5) sts at beg of next 4 rows, continuing in patt as established.

BO 6 (6, 6, 6, 7) sts at beginning of next 2 rows.

Place rem 17 (25, 33, 31, 35) sts on a holder or scrap yarn.

sleeves

(make 2)

CO 33 (35, 37, 39, 41) sts with a single strand on dpns, pm on both sides of center st. Join for working in the round, placing a contrasting marker to note beg of round.

Knit 3 rows.

Inc Round: Inc using **lifted increase** (see "Pattern Notes") in st before first marker and st after second marker. 2 sts increased.

Continue in St st and rep Inc Round every 10th (9th, 8th, 8th, 7th) round 8 (9, 10, 11, 13) more times. 51 (55, 59, 63, 69) sts. You may wish to move to a circular needle as the number of sts increase.

Work in St st until piece measures 18½ (18½, 18½, 18½, 19½)" from cast-on edge, ending with a WS row.

Shape Sleeve Cap

You will work this section back and forth. Start Row 1 at beg of round marker.

Rows 1 and 2: BO 4 (4, 5, 5, 5) sts at beg of next 2 rows. 43 (47, 49, 53, 59) sts.

Rows 3 and 4: BO 2 (2, 3, 3, 3) sts at beg of next 2 rows. 39 (43, 43, 47, 53) sts.

Rows 5 and 6: BO 2 sts at beg of next 2 rows. 35 (39, 39, 43, 49) sts.

Row 7: K1, ssk, k to last 3 sts, k2tog, k1. 33 (37, 37, 41, 47) sts.

Row 8: Purl.

Rep Rows 7 and 8 1 (2, 2, 2, 3) more time(s).

Work 2 (2, 8, 8, 6) rows even. 31 (33, 33, 35, 41) sts.

Rep Rows 7 and 8 10 (10, 9, 10, 11) times. 11 (13, 15, 17, 19) sts.

BO.

finishing

Block all pieces. Using 1 strand of yarn and a tapestry needle, sew shoulder seams. Sew side seams. Sew sleeves into place.

hood

*You will work the hood in St st with 1 strand of yarn. Use the **lifted increase** (see Pattern Notes) to make increases.*

Beg about 3½" below shoulder seam on right front neck, with RS facing, pick up and knit 14 sts to right shoulder, k across 17 (25, 33, 31, 35) held sts for back neck, pick up and knit 14 sts down left front neck. 45 (53, 61, 59, 63) sts. Place markers on both sides of center st.

Next row (WS): Purl.

Next row (RS): Knit, increasing 12 (12, 12, 14, 12) sts evenly across row. 57 (65, 73, 73, 75) sts.

Work 3 rows even in St st.

Inc 1 st on both sides of marked center st every 4th row a total of 9 times. 75 (83, 91, 91, 93) sts.

Continue in St st for another 3 (3, 3¼, 3¼, 3½)" ending on a WS row.

Shape Top of Hood
Next row (RS): K to 3 sts before marker, sk2p, sm, k1, sm, k3tog, k to end.

Next row: Purl.

Rep these 2 rows 4 times. 55 (63, 71, 71, 73) sts.

Next row: K to 2 sts before marker, ssk, sm, k1, sm, k2tog, k to end of row.

Next row: Purl.

Rep these 2 rows 2 times. 51 (57, 65, 65, 67) sts.

Next row: K to marker, remove it, k1, remove marker, k1, pm, k to end.

Next row: P to marker, sm, p3tog, p to end.

Next row: K to 2 sts before marker, k2tog, sm, k to end.

Divide rem sts in half, placing 24 (27, 31, 31, 32) sts on each end of needle. With WS together, join sts using Kitchener st (see "Special Knitting Techniques" appendix).

Re-block sweater as needed. Weave in all ends.

LAKESHORE

openwork cover-up

by Jillian Moreno

Lakeshore is a light and airy tunic that you can wear over a t-shirt for an early morning stroll or over a bathing suit after a day at the beach. (Don't worry. If you use Dream in Color to make this pattern, it's a superwash wool!). An easy-to-memorize lace pattern combined with sock yarn on size US 6 needles make this a quick and satisfying knit. You can wear it with either the boat neck or the deeply scooped neckline in front.

pattern notes

The charts used in this pattern are available for you to download and print at **www.wiley.com/go/knittinginthesun**.

directions

back

CO 98 (110, 118, 128, 138, 148) sts.

Work 4 rows in garter st.

Next row (WS): K1 (1, 5, 4, 3, 2), pm, k96 (106, 108, 120, 132, 144), pm, k1 (1, 5, 4, 3, 2).

Begin working the Lacy Cable patt by following the chart, beginning with Row 1 (a RS row), and keeping the sts outside the markers in St st.

Continue in patt for 27 (27, 27, 29, 29, 29)".

Shape Shoulders and Neck

Work 29 (35, 39, 44, 49, 54) sts in patt for right shoulder, BO center 40 sts, work 29 (35, 39, 44, 49, 54) sts in patt for left shoulder. Put shoulder sts on holder.

front

Work as for Back until piece measures 17 (17, 17, 19, 19, 19)".

SIZE
S (M, L, 1X, 2X, 3X)

FINISHED MEASUREMENTS
Chest circumference: 39 (43, 47, 51, 55, 59)"

Length: 27 (27, 27, 29, 29, 29)"

MATERIALS
- Dream in Color *Smooshy* (100% superwash merino; 450 yd. per 4oz skein); color: 210 Beach Fog; 3 (3, 3, 4, 4, 4) skeins
- US 6 (4mm) straight or circular needles, any length *(or size needed to match gauge)*
- US F (4mm) crochet hook
- Cable needle
- 2 stitch holders
- Stitch markers
- Tapestry needle

GAUGE
20 sts × 24 rows = 4" in St st

SKILLS USED
increasing, decreasing, lace and cable knitting, chart reading, single crochet, thee-needle bind-off

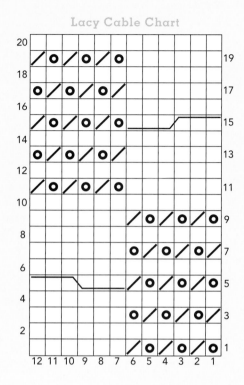

Lacy Cable Chart

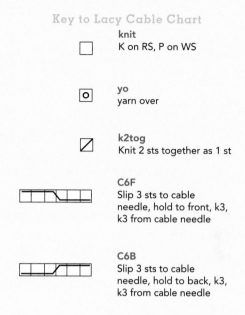

Key to Lacy Cable Chart

knit
K on RS, P on WS

yo
yarn over

k2tog
Knit 2 sts together as 1 st

C6F
Slip 3 sts to cable
needle, hold to front, k3,
k3 from cable needle

C6B
Slip 3 sts to cable
needle, hold to back, k3,
k3 from cable needle

Shape Neck

You will shape both sides of neck at the same time, working with two balls of yarn.

Work 49 (54, 59, 64, 69, 74) sts in patt, attach a second ball of yarn, and work to end of row in patt.

To dec on left front neck: Omit last yo of the row to dec in lacy sections; end rows with k2tog, k1 to dec in cable sections.

To dec on right front neck: Omit first yo of the row in lacy sections; beg row with k1, ssk to dec in cable section.

Stop cables when fewer than 6 sts rem in that section and continue those sts in St st.

Dec every RS row 15 times, then dec every 4th row 5 times. 29 (35, 39, 44, 49, 54) sts for each shoulder.

Work even until piece measures 27 (27, 27, 29, 29, 29)".

Put shoulder sts on holder.

sleeves

(make 2)

CO 94 (94, 104, 104, 114, 114) sts.

Work 4 rows in garter st.

Next row (WS): K5 (5, 4, 4, 3, 3), pm, k84 (84, 96, 96, 108, 108), pm, k5 (5, 4, 4, 3, 3).

Begin Lacy Cable patt from chart, starting with Row 1 (a RS row), and keeping sts outside the markers in St st.

Continue in patt for 12 (13, 14, 15½, 16, 16)".

BO.

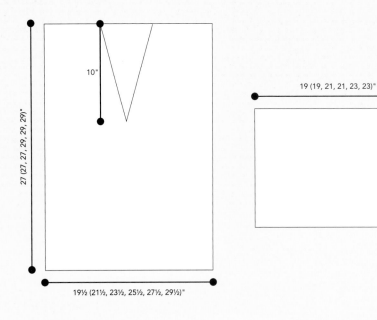

27 (27, 27, 29, 29, 29)"

10"

19½ (21½, 23½, 25½, 27½, 29½)"

19 (19, 21, 21, 23, 23)"

16 (16, 15½, 14, 13, 12)"

finishing

Seam shoulders together with three-needle bind-off (see "Special Knitting Techniques" appendix).

Block to measurements.

Sew on sleeves. Sew side seams, leaving a 4" slit at the hem on each side.

Using crochet hook, single crochet around neck opening and side vents.

Weave in ends.

MONTAGUE
ripple-stitch tunic

by Sarah Barbour

T his long tunic is a great piece to layer over jeans or leggings, or to throw on when a warm day comes to a cooler end. The undulating ribs are eye-catching and fun to work. Combine them with smart shaping at the armholes and a sexy neckline and this cover-up has super, feminine styling that's easy to wear. Even better, the yarn is machine washable, which makes your sunny days truly carefree.

pattern notes

Measuring gauge over Ripple Stitch is tricky because this pattern has a lot of lateral stretch to it. For best results, work a generous swatch and measure after washing and blocking. The yarn used in this pattern has a recommended gauge of 20 stitches per 4".

When working a decrease or bind-off over a yarn over before a drop row (that is, Rows 6 or 12), drop this stitch before decreasing. This stitch does not count as a decreased stitch.

ripple stitch

(multiple of 8 sts + 2)

Preparation Row: (RS): *P2, k1, yo, k1, p2, k2; rep from * to last 2 sts, p2.

Rows 1, 3, and 5 (WS): *K2, p2, k2, p3; rep from * to last 2 sts, k2.

Rows 2 and 4: *P2, k3, p2, k2; rep from * to last 2 sts, p2.

Row 6: *P2, k1, drop next st off needle and unravel down to yo 6 rows below; k1, p2, k1, yo, k1; rep from * to last 2 sts, p2.

Rows 7, 9, and 11: *K2, p3, k2, p2; rep from * to last 2 sts, k2.

Rows 8 and 10: *P2, k2, p2, k3; rep from * to last 2 sts, p2.

Row 12: *P2, k1, yo, k1, p2, k1, drop next st off needle and unravel to yo 6 rows below, k1; rep from * to last 2 sts, p2.

SIZE

S (M, L, 1X, 2X, 3X)

FINISHED MEASUREMENTS

Chest circumference: 32 (36, 40, 43, 50, 54)

To fit chest sizes up to: 34 (38, 42, 46, 50, 54)

Length: 35¼ (35½, 36¼, 36¼, 37½, 37½)

MATERIALS

- Cascade Yarns *Sierra* (80% pima cotton, 20% merino wool; 191 yd. per 100g skein); color: 18 dark pink; 6 (7, 7, 8, 9, 9) skeins.
- US 6 (4mm) straight or circular needles, any length *(or size needed to match gauge)*
- Size G (4.25 mm) crochet hook
- Stitch holder
- Tapestry needle

GAUGE

20 sts × 26 rows = 4" over Ripple Stitch, blocked, unstretched

SKILLS USED

decreasing, drop-stitch pattern

directions

This tunic is knit in Ripple Stitch throughout.

front

Using the long-tail method, CO 72 (80, 88, 96, 112, 120) sts.

Knit 3 rows to create garter st edging.

K3, work the Preparation Row of the Ripple Stitch Pattern to last 3 sts, k3.

Work Rows 1–12 of Ripple Stitch Pattern 3 times, knitting the first and last 3 sts of each row to form garter st edging for the side vents. The piece will measure about 8".

Work Rows 1–11 of the Ripple Stitch Pattern.

Next row: CO 1 st, using backward loop or knitted cast-on, p1, k2, work in patt as established to end of row.

Next row: CO 1 st, k1, p2, work patt as established to end of row.

Continue to work in Ripple Stitch Pattern for 10 full pattern repeats, or until piece measures about 3" shorter than desired length to underarm, ending with Row 12.

Divide Neck

Next Row (Row 1 of patt): Work 41 (47, 50, 56, 65, 68) sts in patt; place these sts on a holder. Work to end of row in patt.

Continuing on the left side only, work Row 2 of patt over 39 (46, 48, 55, 64, 66) sts, k1. Continue working this last st in St st on following rows.

Work Rows 3–12, then Rows 1–11 of Ripple Stitch Pattern.

Shape Armhole and Neck

Read through the following section before continuing; you will shape the armhole and the neckline simultaneously for the two largest sizes.

Next RS row (Row 12 of patt): BO 5 (5, 6, 6, 5, 5) sts, work to end of row.

Work Row 1 in patt.

Next RS row (Row 2 of patt): BO 3 sts, work in patt to end of row.

Continuing to work in patt, dec 1 st at beg of next 3 (4, 4, 4, 8, 9) RS rows.

At the same time, after you work 3 full patt repeats from neckline split, then shape the neck as follows:

Next WS row (Row 1 of patt): BO 9 (10, 11, 12, 13, 14) sts, work to end of row.

Work 1 row in patt.

Next WS row: BO 3 (3, 3, 3, 3, 4) sts, work in patt to end of row.

Next row (Dec Row) (RS): Work in patt to last 4 sts, k2tog, k2.

Rep Dec Row every RS row 3 (7, 7, 6, 7, 9) more times. 13 (14, 15, 21, 25, 23) sts.

Work even until armhole measures 8¼ (8½, 9¼, 9¼, 10½, 10½)".

BO rem sts.

Right Front

Transfer the 41 (47, 50, 56, 65, 68) sts from holder to working needles.

K1, work Row 2 of pattern to end of row. Continue to work first st in St st on following rows.

Work Rows 3–12, then Rows 1–12 of Ripple Stitch Pattern.

Shape Armhole and Neck

Read through the following section before continuing; you will shape the armhole and the neckline simultaneously for the two largest sizes.

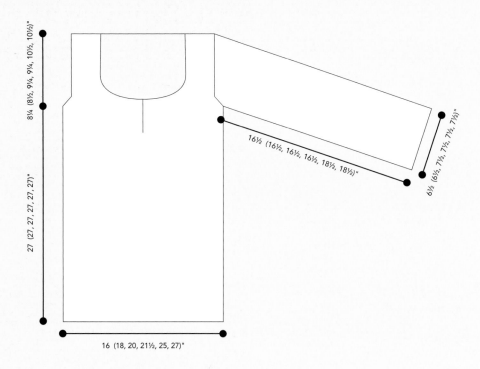

8¼ (8½, 9¼, 9¼, 10½, 10½)"

27 (27, 27, 27, 27, 27)"

16½ (16½, 16½, 16½, 18½, 18½)"

6½ (6½, 7½, 7½, 7½, 7½)"

16 (18, 20, 21½, 25, 27)"

Next WS row (Row 1 of patt): BO 5 (5, 6, 6, 5, 5) sts, work to end of row.

Work Row 1 in patt.

Next WS row (Row 3 of patt): BO 3 sts, work in patt to end of row.

Continuing to work in patt, dec 1 st at end of next 3 (4, 4, 4, 8, 9) RS rows.

At the same time, after you work 3 full patt repeats from neckline split, then shape the neck as follows:

Next RS row (Row 2 of patt): BO 9 (10, 11, 12, 13, 14) sts, work to end of row.

Work 1 row in patt.

Next RS row (Row 4 of patt): BO 3 (3, 3, 3, 3, 4) sts, work in patt to end of row.

Next row (Dec Row) (RS): K2, ssk, work in patt to end of row.

Rep Dec Row every RS row 3 (7, 7, 6, 7, 9) more times. 13 (14, 15, 21, 25, 23) sts.

Work even until armhole measures 8¼ (8½, 9¼, 9¼, 10½, 10½)" or the same as the left front.

BO rem sts.

back

Work as for Front until back measures the same as front to beg of armhole shaping, ending with a WS row.

Next 2 rows: BO 5 (5, 6, 6, 5, 5) sts, work to end of row, maintaining pattern as set.

Next 2 rows: BO 3 sts, work to end of row, maintaining patt.

Dec 1 st at beg and end of next 3 (4, 4, 4, 8, 9) RS rows using k1, ssk at beg of rows and k2tog, k1 at end of rows.

Work even until armholes measure 8¼ (8½, 9¼, 9¼, 10½, 10½)".

BO all sts.

sleeves

(make 2)

CO 66 (66, 74, 74, 74, 74) sts.

Knit 3 rows.

Work the Preparation Row once, then Rows 1–12 of Ripple Stitch Pattern 7 (7, 7, 7, 8, 8) times.

Work Rows 1–11 of Ripple Stitch Pattern.

Shape Sleeve Cap

Maintain Ripple Stitch Pattern as set as you shape the sleeve cap.

BO 5 (5, 6, 6, 5, 5) sts at beg of next 2 rows.

BO 3 sts at beg of next 2 rows.

Dec 1 st at beg and end of every 4th row 3 (3, 4, 4, 6, 6) times, using k1, ssk at beg of rows and k2tog, k1 at end of rows.

Dec 1 st at beg and end of every RS row 10 (11, 11, 11, 11, 11) times.

BO 2 sts at beg of next 2 rows. 20 (18, 22, 22, 20, 20) sts.

BO.

finishing

Weave in ends and block pieces to measurements shown in schematic. If desired, steam fabric from WS to open up the patt for a drapier effect. Sew shoulder seams. Sew sleeves into armholes. Sew sleeve seams and side seams.

make cord for neck

With crochet hook, make a chain 52" long (see "Special Knitting Techniques" appendix). Thread the crocheted cord through the eyelets along the neck split as you would to lace a shoe.

CARDIGANS

QUIMPER
hourglass bolero
by Carol Feller

E ven in warm climates, evenings can get cooler. Fend off the cold shoulder with this bolero jacket. Knit from the top down with raglan sleeves, you can easily modify the size of this bolero by trying it on while you work and adjusting the amount of rows worked.

The square neck closure and hourglass-pattern detailing echo the style of its intended companion, the Anna Maria shell on page 51.

pattern notes

The charts used in this pattern are available for you to download and print at **www.wiley.com/go/knittinginthesun**.

directions

This bolero is knit from the top down in one piece with raglan sleeves. You will increase on both sides of each of the 4 raglan markers to shape the bolero. At the same time, *you will work the hourglass stitch pattern on the top of both sleeves between the contrasting markers. Read through the following sections entirely before you begin knitting.*

collar

Using smaller circular needle, CO 52 (58, 64, 70, 76, 82, 82) sts.

Next row: Kfb, (k1, p1) to end of row to begin Seed Stitch. 53 (59, 65, 71, 77, 83, 83) sts.

Next row: Kfb, then work in Seed Stitch (k in p sts; p in k sts) to end of row. Rep this row 7 more times. 60 (66, 72, 78, 84, 90, 90) sts.

Work 8 rows even in Seed Stitch.

SIZE
XS (S, M, L, 1X, 2X, 3X)

FINISHED MEASUREMENTS
Chest circumference: 29 (34, 38, 42, 46, 50, 54)"
Length: 11½ (12½, 14, 15, 16, 18, 19)"

MATERIALS
- Rowan *Bamboo Soft* (100% bamboo; 112 yd. per 50g ball); color: Cambria; 5 (5, 6, 7, 8, 10, 11) balls
- US 5 (3.75mm) circular needle, 24" or 32" length
- US 4 (3.5mm) circular needle, 24" or 32" length
- US 4 (3.5mm) double-pointed needles *(or size needed to match gauge)*
- US 5 (3.75mm) double-pointed needles
- 8 stitch markers: 4 of one sort, 4 contrasting
- Tapestry needle
- Button

continued ➤

➤ continued

GAUGE

24 sts × 32 rows = 4" in St st on larger needles, unblocked

24 sts × 30 rows = 4" in St st on larger needles, blocked

SKILLS USED

increasing, decreasing, raglan shaping, knitting from charts

yoke

Change to larger circular needle.

Set-up Row (RS): Work 5 sts in Seed Stitch, k2 (3, 5, 6, 8, 10, 9), kfb, place marker (pm), kfb, place contrasting marker, work 7 sts from Single Hourglass Chart, place contrasting marker, kfb, pm, kfb, k24 (28, 30, 34, 36, 38, 40), kfb, pm, kfb, place contrasting marker, work 7 sts from Single Hourglass Chart, place contrasting marker, kfb, pm, kfb, k2 (3, 5, 6, 8, 10, 9), work 5 sts in Seed Stitch. 68 (74, 80, 86, 92, 98, 98) sts.

BEGIN HOURGLASS STITCH PATTERN

You will now work the hourglass stitch pattern as follows between the contrasting markers on both sleeves. Follow these directions for the stitch pattern at the same time as you continue with the pattern shaping below.

Work through the 8 rows of the Single Hourglass Chart 3 (3, 3, 3, 4, 4, 4) times.

After the last round, move both contrasting markers on each sleeve out 3 sts on each side of the patt panels (each patt panel is now 13 sts wide).

On the next row, beg working from the Double Hourglass Chart and purl the 2nd and 12th sts between markers.

Continue working through the 8 rows of the Double Hourglass Chart 3 (3, 3, 3, 4, 4, 4) times.

After the last round, move both contrasting markers out 3 sts on each side of both patt panels (each patt panel is now 19 sts wide).

On the next row, beg working from the Triple Hourglass Chart and purl the 3rd and 17th sts between markers.

Continue working through the 8 rows of the Triple Hourglass Chart 3 (3, 3, 3, 4, 4, 4) times.

After the last round, move both contrasting markers out 3 sts on each side of both patt panels (each patt panel is now 25 sts wide).

On the next row, beg working from the Four Hourglass Chart and purl the 2nd and 25th sts between markers.

Continue working through the 8 rows of the Four Hourglass Chart 3 (3, 3, 3, 4, 4, 4) times.

Continue rep the Four Hourglass Chart as necessary for desired sleeve length.

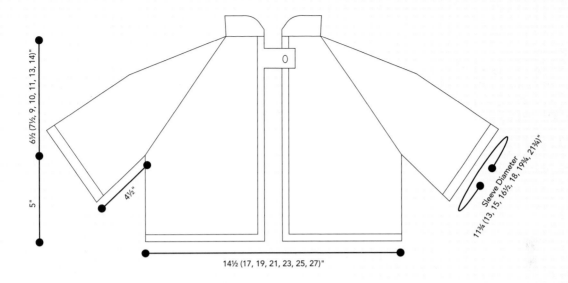

6½ (7½, 9, 10, 11, 13, 14)"

5"

4½"

Sleeve Diameter
11¾ (13, 15, 16½, 18, 19¾, 21¾)"

14½ (17, 19, 21, 23, 25, 27)"

Make Button Band

Next row (WS): CO 18 sts using cable cast-on for the button band, work in Seed Stitch for 23 sts, p to contrasting marker, work panel sts from chart, p to second hourglass patt panel, work panel sts from chart, p to last 5 sts, work in Seed Stitch to end. 86 (92, 98, 104, 110, 116, 116) sts.

Row 1 (RS): Work 5 sts in Seed Stitch, k to last st before marker, kfb, slip marker (sm), kfb, k to hourglass patt panel, work panel sts from chart, k to last st before marker, kfb, sm, kfb, k to last st before marker, kfb, sm, kfb, k to patt panel, work panel sts from chart, k to last st before marker, kfb, sm, kfb, k to last 23 sts, work in Seed Stitch to end. 94 (100, 106, 112, 118, 124, 124) sts.

Row 2 (WS): Work in Seed Stitch for 23 sts, p to hourglass patt panel, work panel sts from chart, p to second hourglass patt panel, work panel sts from chart, p to last 5 sts, work in Seed Stitch to end.

Rep last 2 rows 2 more times. 110 (116, 122, 128, 134, 140, 140) sts.

Buttonhole Row (RS): Work as for Row 1 to last 23 sts, work in Seed Stitch for 18 sts, yo, k2tog, Seed Stitch to end. 118 (124, 130, 136, 142, 148, 148) sts.

Next row (WS): Rep Row 2.

Rep Rows 1 and 2 twice more, then work Row 1 once more. 142 (148, 154, 160, 166, 172, 172) sts.

Finish Button Band (WS): BO 18 sts, work in Seed Stitch for 5 sts, p to hourglass patt panel, work panel sts from chart, p to second hourglass patt panel, work patt panel from chart, p to last 5 sts, work in Seed Stitch to end. 124 (130, 136, 142, 148, 154, 154) sts.

Row 3 (RS): Work 5 sts in Seed Stitch, k to last st before marker, kfb, sm, kfb, k to hourglass patt panel, work panel sts from chart, k to last st before marker, kfb, sm, kfb, k to last st before marker, kfb, sm, kfb, k to patt panel, work panel sts from chart, k to last st before marker, kfb, sm, kfb, k to last 5 sts, work in Seed Stitch to end. 132 (138, 144, 150, 156, 162, 162) sts.

Four Hourglass Chart

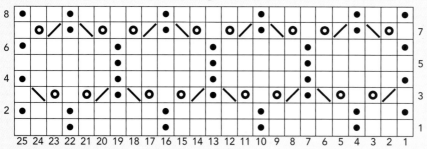

8 7 6 5 4 3 2 1

25 24 23 22 21 20 19 18 17 16 15 14 13 12 11 10 9 8 7 6 5 4 3 2 1

Triple Hourglass Chart

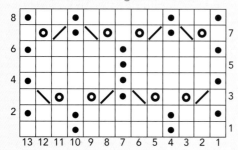

8 7 6 5 4 3 2 1

19 18 17 16 15 14 13 12 11 10 9 8 7 6 5 4 3 2 1

Double Hourglass Chart

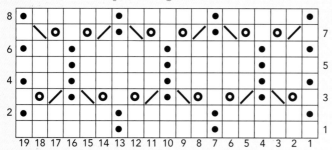

8 7 6 5 4 3 2 1

13 12 11 10 9 8 7 6 5 4 3 2 1

Single Hourglass Chart

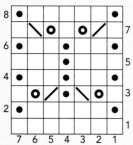

8 7 6 5 4 3 2 1

7 6 5 4 3 2 1

Key to Charts

knit
K on RS, P on WS

purl
P on RS, K on WS

yo
yarn over

k2tog
Knit 2 sts together as 1 st

ssk
Slip 1 st as if to knit, slip another
st as if to knit. Insert LH needle into
front of these 2 sts and knit them together

Row 4 (WS): Work in Seed Stitch for 5 sts, p to hourglass patt panel, work panel sts from chart, p to second patt panel, work panel sts from chart, p to last 5 sts, work in Seed Stitch to end.

Rep last 2 rows 16 (19, 25, 29, 33, 40, 44) more times. 260 (290, 344, 382, 420, 482, 514) sts.

sleeves

Work to first marker in patt. You will continue on the sts for first sleeve only; leave rem sts on the needle.

Transfer 59 (65, 77, 85, 93, 107, 115) sts for sleeve to larger dpns; CO 12 (14, 14, 14, 16, 12, 16) sts using cable or backward loop cast-on, pm for start of round at center of these sts; join to work in the round. 71 (79, 91, 99, 109, 119, 131) sts.

Continue to work the hourglass patt panels as detailed above and rest of sleeve in St st for 3½", or ½" shorter than desired sleeve length.

Switch to smaller dpns and work in Seed Stitch for 6 rounds.

BO in patt.

Transfer 59 (65, 77, 85, 93, 107, 115) sts for second sleeve to larger dpns and work second sleeve the same as the first.

body

Pick up and knit 12 (14, 14, 14, 16, 12, 16) sts from sts cast on at underarm, k76 (86, 100, 112, 122, 138, 148) sts to second underarm, pick up and knit 12 (14, 14, 14, 16, 12, 16) sts from underarm cast-on, k to last 5 sts, work in Seed Stitch to end. 166 (188, 218, 240, 266, 292, 316) sts.

Work even until body measures 4" from underarm, continuing to work first and last 5 sts in Seed Stitch.

Change to smaller circular needle and work 6 rows in Seed Stitch.

BO in patt.

finishing

Weave in all ends. Block to desired dimensions. Sew on button opposite buttonhole.

BRIDGETOWN
lace-paneled cardigan

by Susan Robicheau

This classic cardigan, worked in a pure soy yarn, will take you through all the seasons as a perfect layering piece. Striking lace panels up the fronts and center back add visual interest and knitting fun. The simple stockinette finishes around the collar and button bands keep it fresh and up-to-date. This feminine cardigan goes well with anything in your wardrobe, but pair it with the Bay of Fundy pullover tee (on page 80) to create a terrific twin set.

pattern notes

It's smart to buy buttons *after* completing the cardigan to determine the best size for your buttonholes. Buttons shown have a ¾" diameter.

directions

The body begins with a wide lace border. Once the border is complete, you'll continue in St st with a lovely lace panel up each side of the front and the center back.

back

CO 103 (113, 123, 133, 143, 153) sts.

Border

Row 1 and all other WS rows: Purl.

Row 2 (RS): K1, [ssk] twice, *[yo, k1] 3 times, yo, s2kp, ssk, rep from * to last 8 sts, [yo, k1] 3 times, yo, [k2tog] twice, k1.

Row 4: K1, ssk, *k3, yo, k1, yo, k3, s2kp, rep from * to last 10 sts, k3, yo, k1, yo, k3, k2tog, k1.

Row 6: K1, ssk, *k2, yo, k3, yo, k2, s2kp, rep from * to last 10 sts, k2, yo, k3, yo, k2, k2tog, k1.

SIZE
S (M, L, 1X, 2X, 3X)

FINISHED MEASUREMENTS
Chest circumference: 36 (40, 44, 48, 52, 56)"
Length: 21½ (22, 23, 24, 24½, 25)"

MATERIALS
• SWTC *Pure* (100% Soysilk; 150m per 50g ball), color: 81 Tuscany; 7 (9, 11, 13, 15, 17) balls
• US 6 (4mm) straight or circular needles, any length *(or size needed to match gauge)*
• 4 stitch holders
• 2 stitch markers
• Tapestry needle
• 5 (6, 6, 6, 7, 7) buttons

GAUGE
21 stitches × 26 rows = 4" over St st

SKILLS USED
increasing, decreasing, lace knitting, three-needle bind-off, picking up stitches

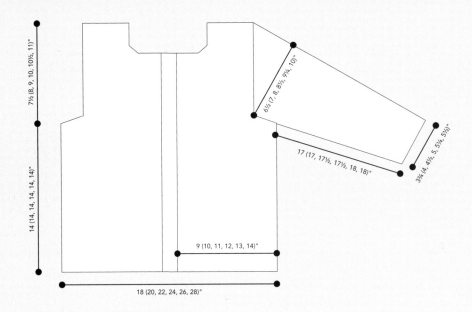

Row 8: K1, ssk, *k1, yo, k5, yo, k1, s2kp, rep from * to last 10 sts, end k1, yo, k5, yo, k1, k2tog, k1.

Row 10: K1, ssk, *yo, k1, yo, ssk, k1, k2tog, yo, k1, yo, s2kp, rep from * ending last rep with k2tog, k1 instead of s2kp.

Row 12: K1, ssk, *yo, k2, yo, s2kp, rep from * to last 5 sts, yo, k2, k2tog, k1.

Row 14: K2, *yo, k3, s2kp, k3, yo, k1, rep from * to last st, k1.

Row 16: K2, *yo, k1, yo, s2kp, ssk, (yo, k1) twice, rep from * to end.

Row 18: K2, *yo, k3, s2kp, k3, yo, k1, rep from * to last st, k1.

Row 20: K3, *yo, k2, s2kp, k2, yo, k3, rep from * to end.

Row 22: K4, *yo, k1, s2kp, k1, yo, k5, rep from *, end last rep k4.

Row 24: K2, *k2tog, yo, k1, yo, s2kp, k1, yo, k1, yo, ssk, k1, rep from *, k1.

Row 26: K1, ssk, *yo, k2, yo, s2kp, rep from * to last 5 sts, yo, k2, yo, k2tog, k1.

Row 28: K1, ssk, *k3, yo, k1, yo, k3, s2kp, rep from * to last 10 sts, k3, yo, k1, yo, k3, k2tog, k1.

Body

Work the Set-up Row once, then begin the Lace Panel Pattern, working the 17-stitch lace panel between the 2 markers.

Set-up Row (WS): K1, p6 (6, 8, 8, 9, 10), p2tog, p12 (14, 15, 17, 19, 20), p2tog, p12 (14, 15, 17, 19, 20), p2tog, p6 (7, 8, 9, 9, 11), pm, k1, p15, k1, pm, p6 (7, 8, 9, 9, 11), p2tog, p12 (14, 15, 17, 19, 20), p2tog, p12 (14, 15, 17, 19, 20), p2tog, p6 (6, 8, 8, 9, 10), k1. 97 (107, 117, 127, 137, 147) sts.

Lace Panel Pattern

Row 1 (RS): K to marker, p1, k1, (k2tog) twice, (yo, k1) 3 times, yo, (ssk) twice, k3, p1, k to end of row.

Rows 2, 4, 6 and 8 (WS): K1, p to marker, k1, p15, k1, p to last st, k1.

Row 3: K to marker, p1, [k2tog] twice, yo, k1, yo, k3, yo, k1, yo, [ssk] twice, k2, p1, k to end of row.

Row 5: K to marker, p1, k3, [k2tog] twice, [yo, k1] 3 times, yo, [ssk] twice, k1, p1, k to end of row.

Row 7: K to marker, p1, k2, [k2tog] twice, yo, k1, yo, k3, yo, k1, yo, [ssk] twice, p1, k to end of row.

Rep these 8 rows 7 more times. The piece will measure about 14". Adjust length to underarm if desired by working more or fewer rows, ending with a WS row.

Shape Armholes
BO 5 (5, 6, 6, 6, 7) sts at beg of next 2 rows.

Next row (RS): K1, k2tog, work in patt to last 4 sts, ssk, k2.

Next row: Work in patt.

Rep last 2 rows 3 (4, 5, 7, 9, 9) more times. 79 (87, 93, 99, 105, 113) sts.

Continue working even in patt until armhole measures 7½ (8, 9, 10, 10½, 11)".

Work across 21 (22, 24, 26, 26, 28) sts, place them on holder for shoulder, BO 37 (43, 45, 47, 53, 57) sts for back neck, work across rem 21 (22, 24, 26, 26, 28) sts, then put them on holder for second shoulder.

right front
CO 53 (53, 63, 73, 73, 83) sts.

Work Border patt as for Back.

Set-up Row (WS): K1, p4 (2, 5, 3, 7, 4), p2tog, p4 (2, 7, 4, 8, 5), p2tog, p5 (2, 6, 4, 8, 5), p0 (2, 0, 2, 0, 2) tog, p0 (2, 6, 4, 0, 5), p0 (2, 0, 2, 0, 2) tog, p0 (2, 0, 4, 0, 5), p0 (2, 0, 0, 0, 0) tog, p0 (2, 0, 0, 0, 0), place marker (pm), k1, p15, k1, pm, p5 (3, 6, 4, 8, 5), p2tog, p4 (2, 7, 4, 8, 5), p2tog, p4 (2, 6, 4, 8, 5), p0 (2, 0, 2, 0, 2) tog, p0 (2, 0, 4, 0, 5), p0 (2, 0, 0, 0, 0) tog, p0 (1, 0, 0, 0, 0), k1. 49 (53, 59, 65, 69, 75) sts.

Beg with Row 1, work 8 rows of Lace Panel as for Back a total of 8 times, then work Row 1 once.

Shape Armhole
Next row (WS): BO 5 (5, 6, 6, 6, 7) sts, work in patt to end of row.

Next row (RS): Work in patt to last 4 sts, ssk, k2.

Next row: Work in patt.

Rep last 2 rows 3 (4, 5, 7, 9, 9) more times. 40 (43, 47, 51, 53, 58) sts.

Continue working even in patt until Right Front measures 5½ (6½, 7½, 7½, 8½, 8½)" from beg of armhole shaping, ending with a WS row.

Shape Neck
Next row (RS): BO 15 (16, 17, 19, 20, 22) sts, work in patt to end of row.

Next row: K1, work in patt to last 3 sts, p2tog, k1.

Next row: K1, ssk, work in patt to end of row.

Rep these 2 rows 2 (3, 4, 4, 5, 6) more times. 21 (22, 24, 26, 26, 28) sts.

Continue in patt until armhole measures 7½ (8, 9, 10, 10½, 11)".

Put sts on holder for shoulder.

left front
Work as for Right Front to armhole shaping, ending with a WS row.

Shape Armhole
Next row (RS): BO 5 (5, 6, 6, 6, 7) sts, work in patt to end of row.

Next row: Work in patt.

Next row: K2, k2tog, work in patt to end of row.

Rep last 2 rows 3 (4, 5, 7, 9, 9) more times. 40 (43, 47, 51, 53, 58) sts.

Continue working even in patt until Left Front measures 5½ (6½, 7½, 7½, 8½, 8½)" from beg of armhole shaping, ending with a RS row.

Shape Neck
Next row (WS): BO 15 (16, 17, 19, 20, 22) sts, work in patt to end of row.

Next row: K1, work in patt to last 3 sts, k2tog, k1.

Next row: K1, p2tog, work in patt to end of row.

Rep last 2 rows 2 (3, 4, 4, 5, 6) more times. 21 (22, 24, 26, 26, 28) sts.

Continue in patt until armhole measures 7½ (8, 9, 10, 10½, 11)".

Put sts on holder for shoulder.

sleeves

(make 2)

CO 39 (43, 47, 51, 55, 59) sts.

Lace Edging
Rows 1, 3, 5, and 7 (WS): K1, p10 (12, 14, 16, 18, 20), k1, p15, k1, p10 (12, 14, 16, 18, 20), k1.

Row 2: K11 (13, 15, 17, 19, 21), p1, k1, [k2tog] twice, [yo, k1] 3 times, yo, [ssk] twice, k3, p1, k to end of row.

Row 4: K11 (13, 15, 17, 19, 21), p1, [k2tog] twice, yo, k1, yo, k3, yo, k1, yo, [ssk] twice, k2, p1, k to end of row.

Row 6: K11 (13, 15, 17, 29, 21), p1, k3, [k2tog] twice, [yo, k1] 3 times, yo, [ssk] twice, k1, p1, k to end of row.

Row 8: K11 (13, 15, 17, 19, 21), p1, k2, [k2tog] twice, yo, k1, yo, k3, yo, k1, yo, [ssk] twice, p1, k to end of row.

Rep Rows 1–8 once more.

Next row (WS): K1, p to last st, k1.

Next row: Knit.

Rep these 2 rows, and, at the same time, shape the sleeve.

Beg with Row 3, inc at beg and end of every 6th row 15 (12, 10, 8, 0, 0) times, then every 4th row 0 (4, 8, 11, 21, 23) times, by beg rows with kfb and ending rows with kfb, k1. 69 (75, 83, 89, 97, 105) sts.

Work even until sleeve measures 17 (17, 17½, 17½, 18, 18)" from cast-on edge, or desired length, ending with a WS row.

Shape Sleeve Cap
BO 5 (5, 6, 6, 6, 7) sts at beg of next 2 rows.

Next row: K2, k2tog, k to last 4 sts, ssk, k2.

Next row: K1, p to last st, k1.

Rep last 2 rows 18 (20, 22, 24, 27, 29) more times. 19 (21, 23, 25, 28, 30) sts.

BO.

finishing

Using the three-needle bind-off (see "Special Knitting Techniques" appendix), join fronts and back at shoulders.

neckband

With RS facing, pick up and knit 15 (16, 17, 19, 20, 22) sts from right front neck, 10 (11, 13, 13, 15, 16) sts along right neck edge, 37 (43, 45, 47, 53, 57) sts along back neck, 10 (11, 13, 13, 15, 16) sts along left neck edge, and 15 (16, 17, 19, 20, 22) sts from left front neck. 87 (97, 105, 111, 123, 133) sts.

Knit 1 WS row.

Work 5 rows in St st, beg with a knit row.

Knit 2 rows.

BO.

buttonhole band

Row 1: Pick up and knit 96 (100, 106, 106, 112, 112) sts along right front edge.

Row 2: Knit 1 WS row.

Rows 3 and 4: Work 2 rows in St st, starting with a knit row.

Row 5: Knit, making 5 (6, 6, 6, 7, 7) buttonholes, evenly spaced, along band as follows: K9 (9, 7, 7, 7, 7), *yo, k2tog, k17 (14, 16, 16, 14, 14), rep from * 4 (5, 5, 5, 6, 6) times, yo, k2tog, k9 (9, 7, 7, 7, 7).

Rows 6 and 7: Work 2 rows in St st, starting with a purl row.

Row 8: Knit 1 WS row.

BO.

button band

Work the same as the Buttonhole Band, but omit the buttonholes on Row 5.

Sew side seams and sleeve seams.

Sew sleeves into armholes.

Sew on buttons opposite buttonholes.

Weave in ends and block.

CORONADO

shawl-collared cardigan

by Kristi Porter

I love the wrap-style cardigan and wanted to create something wearable, stylish, and suitable for those in-between days when the weather is unpredictable. Coronado features a nicely tailored sleeve and waist shaping to provide a comfortable and feminine fit. The fine-gauge yarn ensures that the cardigan isn't bulky, while the eyelet ribbing provides ventilation as well as dynamic lines. You can wear the generous shawl collar in several ways: leave it open to get an artsy, slouchy drape; or close it asymmetrically or double-breasted and secure with a pin to form a broad middy collar.

directions

You will work this cardigan in the Eyelet Rib Pattern throughout with garter-stitch edging.

back

CO 89 (99, 109, 119, 129) sts.

Knit 4 rows to create garter st edging.

Beg working in Eyelet Rib Pattern as follows:

> Row 1 (RS): K3, *yo, s2kp, yo, k5; rep from * to last 6 sts, yo, s2kp, yo, k3.

> Row 2 (WS): Purl.

> Rep these 2 rows to create Eyelet Rib Pattern.

Work even in patt for 1", ending with a WS row.

Shape Waist
Next row (RS): K1, ssk, *yo, s2kp, yo, k5, rep from *, to last 3 sts, k2tog, k1.

Work 3 rows in patt.

SIZE

S (M, L, 1X, 2X)

FINISHED MEASUREMENTS

Chest circumference (with front lapels overlapped): 40 (44, 48, 52, 56)"

Length: 24 (24½, 25, 25½, 26)"

MATERIALS

- SWTC *Inspiration* (50% alpaca, 50% Soysilk; 124 yd. per 50g skein); color: 396 Be Real; 10 (11, 12, 13, 14) skeins
- US 6 (4mm) straight or circular needles, any length *(or size needed to match gauge)*
- 4 small stitch holders or large safety pins
- Tapestry needle

GAUGE

20 sts × 26 rows = 4" over Eyelet Rib Pattern, blocked

SKILLS USED

increasing, decreasing, simple lacework, short rows, three-needle bind-off

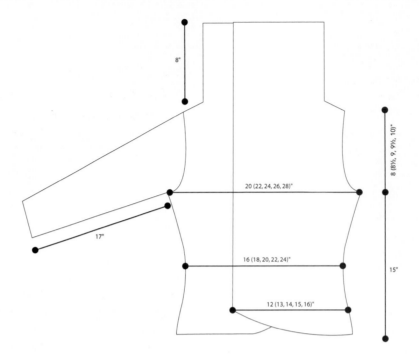

8"

8 (8½, 9, 9½, 10)"

20 (22, 24, 26, 28)"

17"

16 (18, 20, 22, 24)"

15"

12 (13, 14, 15, 16)"

Next row (RS): K2, s2kp, yo, k5, *yo, s2kp, yo, k5, rep from * to last 5 sts, yo, s2kp, k2.

Next row (WS): Purl.

Next row: K9, *yo, s2kp, yo, k5, rep from *, end k9.

Next row: Purl.

Next row: K1, ssk, k6, *yo, s2kp, yo, k5, rep from *, end k6, k2tog, k1.

Work 3 rows in patt.

Next row (RS): K1, ssk, k5, *yo, s2kp, yo, k5, rep from *, end k2tog, k1.

Work 3 rows in patt.

Next row (RS): K1, ssk, k4, *yo, s2kp, yo, k5, rep from *, end k2tog, k1. 79 (89, 99, 109, 119) sts.

Continue working even in patt until Back measures 7 (7, 7½, 7½, 8)", ending with a WS row.

Remember to measure straight along a column of sts rather than along the edge where the waist shaping will skew your measurements.

Inc at each end of the next row as follows:

Inc row (RS): K1, m1, continue in patt to last st, m1, k1.

Rep the Inc Row every following 4th row 9 more times and when 10 plain knit sts are on each end of the needle, add in lace repeats as follows: k2, *yo, s2kp, yo, k5*, yo, s2kp, yo, k2.

At end of waist shaping, there are 99 (109, 119, 129, 139) sts.

Work even until Back measures 15" (for all sizes), ending with a WS row.

Shape Armholes
BO 5 (6, 7, 9, 11) sts at beg of next 2 rows.

Dec 1 st at armhole on both sides every RS row 5 (6, 8, 10, 12) times. 79 (85, 89, 91, 93) sts. (Dec by omitting first and last yarn overs of a row, or by starting a row with k1, ssk and ending a row with k2tog, k1 as you did for the waist shaping.)

Work even until Back measures 8 (8½, 9, 9½, 10)" from beg of armhole shaping, ending with a WS row.

Shape Shoulders

You will shape the shoulders with short rows.

Next row (RS): Work in patt to last 3 (4, 4, 4, 5) sts, wrap next st and turn.

Next row (WS): Purl to last 3 (4, 4, 4, 5) sts, wrap next st and turn.

Next row: Work in patt to last 3 (3, 4, 4, 4) sts, wrap next st and turn.

Next row: Purl to last 3 (3, 4, 4, 4) sts, wrap next st and turn.

Next row: Work in patt to last 2 (3, 4, 4, 4) sts, wrap next st and turn.

Next row: Purl to last 2 (3, 4, 4, 4) sts, wrap next st and turn.

Next row: Work in patt to last 2 (3, 3, 4, 4) sts, wrap next st and turn.

Next row: Purl to last 2 (3, 3, 4, 4) sts, wrap next st and turn.

Next row: Work across in patt, picking up wraps and knitting them together with wrapped sts.

Next row: Purl across, picking up remaining wraps and purling them together with wrapped sts.

Place 10 (13, 15, 16, 17) sts for each shoulder on holders. (Later you will BO the shoulders with the three-needle bind-off.)

Work even on remaining 59 sts (all sizes) for 8". Knit 4 rows to create garter-st edging. BO all sts loosely.

left front

CO 57 (65, 73, 73, 81) sts.

Knit 4 rows to create garter-st edging.

Begin working in Eyelet Rib Pattern as follows (2 edge sts are always knit to create a non-rolling edge):

Row 1 (RS): K3, *yo, s2kp, yo, k5, rep from * to last 6 sts, yo, s2kp, yo, k3.

Row 2 (WS): K2, p to end of row.

Rep these 2 rows until piece measures 1".

Shape Hem and Waist

You will now create a slightly curved bottom edge using short rows. Each short row is 8 sts (1 patt rep) longer than the previous one; you will turn and wrap at the center st of the group of 5 knit sts in each rep. In following rows, when you encounter a wrapped st, pick up the wrap and knit it together with the wrapped st to avoid creating holes. You should slip the first stitch purlwise after you wrap and turn to create a smoother transition between short rows. At the same time, you will dec every 4th row a total of 5 times to shape the waist. Instructions for the short rows and waist decreases are written out line by line below.

Row 1 (RS) (Dec Row): K1, ssk, *yo, s2kp, yo, k5*, rep from * 1 (1, 2, 2, 2) more time(s), yo, s2kp, yo, k2, wrap next st and turn.

Row 2 (WS): Sl 1, p to end of row.

Row 3: K2, *yo, s2kp, yo, k5, rep from * 2 (2, 3, 3, 3) more times, yo, s2kp, yo, k2, wrap next st and turn.

Row 4: Sl 1, p to end of row.

Row 5 (Dec Row): K2, s2kp, yo, k5, *yo, s2kp, yo, k5, rep from * 2 (2, 3, 3, 3) more times, yo, s2kp, yo, k2, wrap next st and turn.

Row 6: Sl 1, p to end of row.

Row 7: K9, *yo, s2kp, yo, k5, rep from * 3 (3, 4, 4, 4) more times, yo, s2kp, yo, k2, wrap next st and turn.

Row 8: Sl 1, p to end of row.

Size S Only:

Row 9 (Dec Row): K1, ssk, k6, *yo, s2kp, yo, k5, rep from * to last 6 sts, yo, s2kp, yo, k3.

Row 10: K2, p to end of row.

Short-row shaping is complete for your size. Continue working on all sts at Row 13.

All Other Sizes:

Row 9 (Dec Row): K1, ssk, k6, *yo, s2kp, yo, k5, rep from * – (4, 5, 5, 5) more times, yo, s2kp, yo, k2, wrap next st and turn.

Row 10: Sl 1, p to end of row.

Sizes M, L, and 1X:

Row 11: K8, *yo s2kp, yo, k5, rep from * to last 6 sts, yo, s2kp, yo, k3.

Row 12: K2, p to end of row.

Short-row shaping is complete for your size. Continue working on all sts at Row 13.

Size 2X Only:

Row 11: K8, *yo, s2kp, yo, k5, rep from * 6 more times, yo, s2kp, yo, k2, wrap next st and turn.

Row 12: Sl 1, p to end of row.

Short-row shaping is complete for your size. Continue working on all sts at Row 13.

All Sizes:

Row 13 (Dec Row): K1, ssk, k5, *yo, s2kp, yo, k5, rep from * to last 6 sts, yo, s2kp, yo, k3.

Row 14: K2, p to end of row.

Row 15: K7, *yo, s2kp, yo, k5, rep from * to last 6 sts, yo, s2kp, yo, k3.

Row 16: K2, p to end of row.

Row 17 (Dec Row): K1, ssk, k4, *yo, s2kp, yo, k5, rep from * to last 6 sts, yo, s2kp, yo k3. 52 (60, 68, 68, 76) sts.

Continue working even in patt until Left Front measures 7 (7, 7½, 7½, 8)", ending with a WS row.

Inc at beg of next row as follows:

> Inc row (RS): K1, m1, continue in patt to end of row.

Work 3 rows even in patt remembering to k first 2 sts of WS rows.

Rep these 4 rows 9 more times and when 10 plain knit sts are at beg of row, add in another Eyelet Rib Pattern rep as follows: k2, *yo, s2kp, yo, k5, rep from * to last 6 sts, yo, s2kp, yo, k3. 62 (70, 78, 78, 86) sts.

Work even until Left Front measures 15" (for all sizes), or the same as Back, ending with a WS row.

Shape Armhole

BO 5 (6, 7, 9, 11) sts at beg of next RS row and continue in patt.

Dec 1 st at armhole on every RS row 5 (6, 8, 10, 12) times, decreasing as you did for the back. 52 (58, 63, 59, 63) sts.

Work even until Left Front measures 8 (8½, 9, 9½, 10)" from beg of armhole shaping, ending with a RS row.

Shape Shoulder

Next row (WS): Purl to last 3 (4, 4, 4, 5) sts, wrap next st and turn.

Next row (RS): Work in patt across.

Next row: Purl to last 6 (7, 8, 8, 9) sts, wrap next st and turn.

Next row: Work in patt across.

Next row: Purl to last 8 (10, 12, 12, 13) sts, wrap next st and turn.

Next row: Work in patt across.

Next row: Purl to last 10 (13, 15, 16, 17) sts, wrap next st and turn.

Next row: Work in patt across.

Next row: Purl across, picking up rem wraps and purling them together with wrapped sts.

Place 10 (13, 15, 16, 17) sts for shoulder on a holder for later three-needle bind off.

Work even on remaining 42 (45, 48, 43, 46) sts for 8". Knit 4 rows to create garter-st edging. BO all sts loosely.

right front

CO 57 (65, 73, 73, 81) sts.

Knit 4 rows to create garter-st edging.

Beg working in Eyelet Rib Pattern as follows:

> Row 1 (RS): K3, *yo, s2kp, yo, k5, rep from * to last 6 sts, yo, s2kp, yo, k3.

> Row 2 (WS): Purl to last 2 sts, k2. Continue making this 2-st border as you did on Left Front.

Rep these 2 rows until piece measures 1".

Shape Hem and Waist

Next row (RS) (Dec Row): K3, *yo, s2kp, yo, k5*, rep from * to last 3 sts, k2tog, k1.

Dec 1 st at end of row every 4th row 4 more times and at the same time *beg short-row shaping as follows:*

Next row (WS): Purl 23 (23, 31, 31, 31), wrap the next st and turn.

Next row (RS): Sl 1, work in patt to end of row.

Next row: Purl to wrapped st, pick up wrap and p it together with wrapped st, p7, wrap next st and turn.

Rep these 2 rows 3 (4, 4, 4, 5) times. Then continue on all sts, knitting the last 2 sts on WS rows to form edging. The short-row shaping is now complete.

Continue waist decs as necessary for your size. 52 (60, 68, 68, 76) sts.

Continue working even in patt until Right Front measures 7 (7, 7½, 7½, 8)", ending with a WS row.

Inc at beg of next row as follows:

> Inc row (RS): K1, m1, continue in patt to end of row.

Work 3 rows even in patt, remembering to k last 2 sts of WS rows.

Rep these 4 rows 9 more times and when 10 plain knit sts are at end of row, add in another Eyelet Rib Pattern rep as follows: k3, *yo, s2kp, yo, k5, rep from * to last 5 sts, yo, s2kp, yo, k2. 62 (70, 78, 78, 86) sts.

Work even until Right Front measures 15" (for all sizes), or the same as the Back, ending with a WS row.

Shape Armhole

BO 5 (6, 7, 9, 11) sts at beg of next WS row and continue in patt.

Dec 1 st at armhole on every RS row 5 (6, 8, 10, 12) times, decreasing as you did for the back. 52 (58, 63, 59, 63) sts.

Work even until Right Front measures 8 (8½, 9, 9½, 10)" from beg of armhole shaping, ending with a WS row.

Shape Shoulder

Next row (RS): Work in patt to last 3 (4, 4, 4, 5) sts, wrap next st and turn.

Next row (WS): Purl.

Next row: Work in patt to last 6 (7, 8, 8, 9) sts, wrap next st and turn.

Next row: Purl.

Next row: Work in patt to last 8 (10, 12, 12, 13) sts, wrap next st and turn.

Next row: Purl.

Next row: Work in patt to last 10 (13, 15, 16, 17) sts, wrap next st and turn.

Next row: Purl.

Next row: Work in patt across, picking up remaining wraps and knitting them together with wrapped sts.

Place 10 (13, 15, 16, 17) sts for shoulder on a holder for later three-needle bind-off.

Work even on remaining 42 (45, 48, 43, 46) sts for 8". Knit 4 rows to create garter-st edging. BO all sts loosely.

join shoulders

With RS together and WS facing out, join shoulders using three-needle bind-off (see "Special Knitting Techniques" appendix).

sleeves

(make 2)

CO 41 (41, 49, 49, 49) sts.

Knit 4 rows to create garter-st edging.

Beg working in Eyelet Rib Pattern as follows:

> Row 1 (RS): K3, *yo, s2kp, yo, k5, rep from * to last 6 sts, yo, s2kp, yo, k3.

> Row 2 (WS): Purl.

Inc 1 st at each side every 10th (10th, 10th, 8th, 6th) row 8 (11, 10, 13, 16) times. 57 (63, 69, 75, 81) sts. Add patt reps when 10 plain knit sts are at each end of needle as you did on Left and Right Fronts.

Work even until sleeve measures 17", or desired length to underarm.

Shape Sleeve Cap

BO 5 (6, 7, 9, 11) sts at beg of next 2 rows. 47 (51, 55, 57, 59) sts.

Dec 1 st at each edge every RS row 14 (16, 18, 19, 20) times, decreasing as you did for the back. 19 sts.

BO 2 sts at beg of next 4 rows.

BO rem 11 sts.

finishing

Block pieces to measurements given on schematic.

Sew sleeve caps to body. Sew side and sleeve seams. Weave in ends.

SAINT AUGUSTINE

tube-sleeved shrug

by Tonya Wagner

We all have them—cute tube tops, camisoles, and sundresses that are perfect for warm days of shopping, lunch with friends, and walking around the neighborhood. But then night falls or you go inside a cool movie theater and your favorite tank top isn't so cute when you get goose bumps.

Enter Saint Augustine. This lightweight shrug is a simple design so it doesn't distract from what you're wearing. Though the yarn contains alpaca and wool, it is knit at a loose gauge so it doesn't get too warm. Saint Augustine is a top-down raglan with absolutely no seaming. There are no arm decreases; the knitter switches to smaller needles to create the wide ribbed cuffs. This creates a loose-fitting sleeve inspired by the slouchy boots popular in the '80s. The slouchy effect is emphasized when you push the long sleeves up to three-quarter length.

directions
body

Using larger 24" circular needle, CO 35 (40, 45, 50, 50, 55) sts.

Set-up Row (WS): P7 (8, 9, 10, 10, 11), place marker (pm), p21 (24, 27, 30, 30, 33), pm, p7 (8, 9, 10, 10, 11). Sts between markers will be back of garment; sts on either side will be sleeves.

Row 1 (RS): Kfb, *k to 1 st before marker, kfb, slip marker (sm), kfb, rep from *, k to last 2 sts, kfb, k1. 6 sts increased.

Row 2 (WS): Purl.

Rep last 2 rows 22 (22, 23, 24, 25, 26) times. 173 (178, 189, 200, 206, 217) sts: 53 (54, 57, 60, 62, 65) sts for each sleeve and 67 (70, 75, 80, 82, 87) sts for back.

SIZE
XS (S, M, L, 1X, 2X)

FINISHED MEASUREMENTS
Back width: 16½ (17½, 18¾, 20, 20½, 21¾)"

Length: 9 (9¼, 9½, 9¾, 9¾, 10)"

MATERIALS
- Cascade Yarns *Dolce* (55% super-fine alpaca, 23% silk, 22% wool; 109 yd. per 50g skein); color: 943; 5 (5, 5, 6, 6, 7) skeins

- US 10 (6mm) circular needle, 24" length (*or size needed to match gauge*)

continued ➤

Next row (RS): Using 16" circular needle, k to first marker. Hold rem sts on 24" circular needle, or transfer them to scrap yarn if preferred.

sleeves

Working on the 53 (54, 57, 60, 62, 65) sts on 16" needle only, CO 3 (4, 3, 4, 4, 3) sts using knitted or backward loop cast-on, pm, CO 4 sts, then join to knit in the round.

Knit even in the round until sleeve measures 12½ (13, 13, 13½, 13½, 14)" from cast-on at underarm. Switch to smaller dpns. Work 3" in k1, p1 rib.

BO in rib.

With RS facing and 16" circular needle, rejoin yarn sts held for second sleeve; leave sts for back on 24" needle or scrap yarn. Work the second sleeve the same as the first.

➤ continued

- US 10 (6mm) circular needle, 16" length
- US 7 (4.5mm) circular needle, 24" length
- US 3 (3.25mm) double-pointed needles
- Scrap yarn (optional)
- 2 stitch markers
- Tapestry needle

GAUGE

16 sts × 20 rows = 4" in St st on largest needle

SKILLS USED

increasing, raglan shaping, knitting in the round, picking up stitches

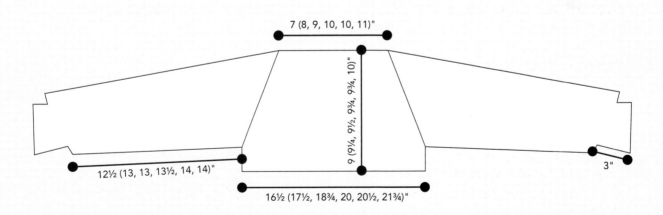

7 (8, 9, 10, 10, 11)"

9 (9¼, 9½, 9¾, 9¾, 10)"

12½ (13, 13, 13½, 14, 14)"

16½ (17½, 18¾, 20, 20½, 21¾)"

3"

back

With RS facing, rejoin yarn to 67 (70, 75, 80, 82, 87) sts on larger 24" circular needle.

Work in St st until back measures 9 (9¼, 9½, 9¾, 9¾, 10)" from cast-on edge, ending with a WS row.

Switch to smaller 24" circular needle and knit 1 row.

Without turning, pick up and knit 30 (31, 32, 33, 33, 34) sts under arm and up first raglan, pick up and knit 35 (40, 45, 50, 50, 55) sts in the sts cast on for neck and tops of sleeves, pick up and knit 30 (31, 32, 33, 33, 34) sts along second raglan and under arm. 162 (172, 184, 196, 198, 210) sts. Mark beg of round.

Work in k1, p1 rib for 1".

BO loosely.

finishing

Weave in ends and block.

YEHLIU

cables-and-lace cardigan

by Anne Kuo Lukito

This airy cardigan, worked in a subtly hand-dyed wool-and-silk blend, will definitely turn heads with its beautiful combination of cables, lace, and openwork. The unusual construction allows the pattern to flow uninterrupted from the cuff across the bodice, making this sweater loads of fun to knit.

pattern notes

When knitting in the round, read all rows of the chart from right to left. When knitting back and forth, read RS rows from right to left and WS rows from left to right.

To assess your gauge over the cables-and-lace pattern, work through the 10 rows of the 29-stitch Chart A1 twice. Washed and blocked, this piece should measure about 7" wide by 3½" tall.

The charts used in this pattern are available for you to download and print at **www.wiley.com/go/knittinginthesun**.

m1

The "make 1" technique that provides the most inconspicuous increases in this pattern is to knit into the stitch in the row below the stitch on the LH needle, then knit the stitch on the LH needle.

directions

You will begin the cardigan at the left cuff and work in the round to the underarm. Then you will divide the piece to work the front and then the back. You will make a second piece for the right side, then join the two pieces at the center back and side seams. After you join the pieces, you will pick up and knit down to the hem in one piece. Finally, you will knit the ribbed band around the front and collar to complete the cardigan.

SIZE
S (M, L, 1X, 2X)

FINISHED MEASUREMENTS
Chest circumference: 32 (38, 44, 50, 56)"
Length: 22 (23, 23½, 24, 24)"

MATERIALS
- Lorna's Laces *Lion and Lamb* (50% silk, 50% wool; 205 yd. per 100g skein); color: Periwinkle; 7 (7, 8, 8, 9) skeins.
- US 8 (5mm) circular needle, 16" length (*or size needed to match gauge*)
- US 8 (5mm) circular needle, 24" or longer
- US 7 (4.5mm) circular needle, 32" or longer
- Stitch holders or scrap yarn
- Stitch markers
- Tapestry needle

GAUGE
17 sts × 23 rows = 4" in St st
17 sts × 23 rows = 4" over cables-and-lace pattern
(*Wash and block swatches before measuring.*)

continued ➤

left side

Sleeve

CO 58 (58, 58, 66, 66) sts using 16" circular needle, join for working in the round, being careful not to twist sts. Place marker (pm) to indicate beg of round.

Set-up Round: *P1 (1, 1, 2, 2), k3, p2 (2, 2, 3, 3), k8, p2 (2, 2, 3, 3), k3, p2 (2, 2, 3, 3), k7, p1, rep from * once.

Beg working from Chart A1 (A1, A1, A2, A2) with Round 1. You will work the 29 (29, 29, 33, 33) sts of the chart twice each round.

Continue working from chart until Rows 1–10 have been worked 6 (7, 7, 8, 8) times.

Shape Underarm

Round 1: Work Row 1 of Chart A1 (A1, A1, A2, A2) twice, inc with pfb in first and last st of the round. 60 (60, 60, 68, 68) sts.

Round 2: P1, work Row 2 of Chart A1 (A1, A1, A2, A2) twice, p1.

➤ continued

SKILLS USED
increasing, decreasing, lace knitting, cabling without a cable needle, knitting in the round, reading charts, unconventional construction

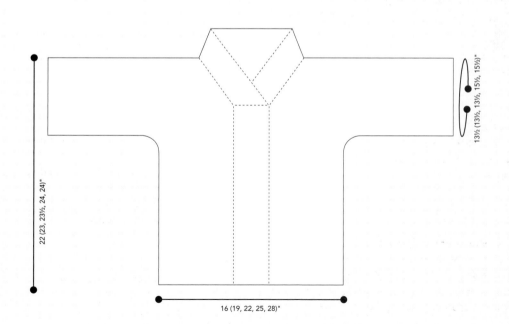

22 (23, 23½, 24, 24)"

13½ (13½, 13½, 15½, 15½)"

16 (19, 22, 25, 28)"

Chart A1

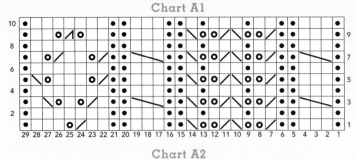

Chart A2

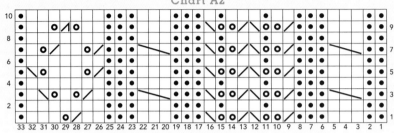

Chart B1

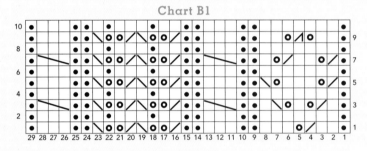

Chart B2

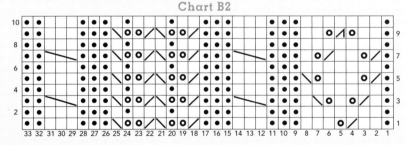

Key to Cables-and-Lace Charts

knit
K on RS, P on WS

purl
P on RS, K on WS

yo
yarn over

k2tog
Knit 2 sts together as 1 st

ssk
Slip 1 st as if to knit, slip another st as if to knit. Insert LH needle into front of these 2 sts and knit them together

k3tog
Knit 3 sts together as 1 st

3-Stitch Twist
Knit the third st on the LH needle, then the second st, then the first st; slip all 3 sts off the LH needle

Round 3: Pfb, work Row 3 of Chart A1 (A1, A1, A2, A2) twice, pfb. 62 (62, 62, 70, 70) sts.

Round 4: K1, p1, work Row 4 of Chart A1 (A1, A1, A2, A2) twice, p1, k1.

Round 5: K1, m1, p1, work Row 5 of Chart A1 (A1, A1, A2, A2) twice, p1, m1, k1. 64 (64, 64, 72, 72) sts.

Round 6: K2, p1, work Row 6 of Chart A1 (A1, A1, A2, A2) twice, p1, k2.

Round 7: K1, m1, k1, p1, work Row 7 of Chart A1 (A1, A1, A2, A2) twice, p1, k1, m1, k1. 66 (66, 66, 74, 74) sts.

Round 8: K3, p1, work Row 8 of Chart A1 (A1, A1, A2, A2) twice, p1, k3.

Round 9: K3, p1, work Row 9 of Chart A1 (A1, A1, A2, A2) twice, p1, k3, CO 5 (5, 5, 7, 7) sts using backward loop cast-on, turn. 71 (71, 71, 81, 81) sts.

You will now work back and forth.

Row 10: P8 (8, 8, 10, 10), k1, work Row 10 of Chart A1 (A1, A1, A2, A2) twice, p2, CO 5 (5, 7, 7) sts using backward loop cast-on, turn. 76 (76, 76, 88, 88) sts.

Upper Bodice
Row 1: K8 (8, 8, 10, 10), p1, work Row 1 of Chart A1 (A1, A1, A2, A2) twice, p1, k8 (8, 8, 10, 10), CO 20 (20, 20, 22, 22) sts using backward loop cast-on, turn. Switch to longer circular needle if desired.

Row 2: Work Row 2 of Chart A1 (A1, A1, A2, A2) 3 times, k1, p8 (8, 8, 10, 10), CO 20 (20, 20, 22, 22) sts.

Row 3: Work Row 3 of Chart A1 (A1, A1, A2, A2) 4 times.

Work Rows 4–10 of Chart A1 (A1, A1, A2, A2), working chart 4 times in each row.

Work Rows 1–10 of Chart A1 (A1, A1, A2, A2) 2 (3, 4, 5, 6) more times.

Shape Neck and Left Front
Row 1: Work Row 1 of Chart A1 (A1, A1, A2, A2) twice, BO 5 (5, 5, 7, 7) sts, p1, (k2tog, yo2, ssk) twice, p2 (2, 2, 3, 3), k3, p2 (2, 2, 3, 3), k2, k2tog, yo, k3, p1, work Row 1 of Chart A1 (A1, A1, A2, A2).

Row 2: Work Row 2 of Chart A1 (A1, A1, A2, A2), k1, p7, k2 (2, 2, 3, 3), p3, k2 (2, 2, 3, 3), (p1, k1, p2) twice, k1; put rem 58 (58, 58, 66, 66) sts on holder for left back.

Row 3: Skp, BO 3 sts, k1, k2tog, yo2, ssk, p2 (2, 2, 3, 3), 3-St Twist, p2 (2, 2, 3, 3), k1, k2tog, yo, k1, yo, ssk, k1, p1, work Row 3 of Chart A1 (A1, A1, A2, A2).

Row 4: Work Row 4 of Chart A1 (A1, A1, A2, A2), k1, p7, k2 (2, 2, 3, 3), p3, k2 (2, 2, 3, 3), p1, k1, p3.

Row 5: Skp, BO 3 (3, 3, 4, 4) sts, p2, k3, p2 (2, 2, 3, 3), k2tog, yo, k3, yo, ssk, p1, work Row 5 of Chart A1 (A1, A1, A2, A2).

Row 6: Work Row 6 of Chart A1 (A1, A1, A2, A2), k1, p7, k2 (2, 2, 3, 3), p3, k3.

Row 7: P3, 3-St Twist, p2 (2, 2, 3, 3), k2tog, yo, k2, k2tog, yo, k1, p1, work Row 7 of Chart A1 (A1, A1, A2, A2).

Row 8: Work Row 8 of Chart A1 (A1, A1, A2, A2), k1, p7, k2 (2, 2, 3, 3), p3, k3.

Row 9: Skp, p1 (1, 1, 2, 2), k3, p2 (2, 2, 3, 3), k2, yo, k3tog, yo, k3, p1, work Row 9 of Chart A1 (A1, A1, A2, A2).

Row 10: Work Row 10 of Chart A1 (A1, A1, A2, A2), k1, p7, k2 (2, 2, 3, 3), p3, k2.

Cut yarn, leaving tail for weaving in later. Place all sts on holder.

Left Back
Transfer 58 (58, 58, 66, 66) sts from holder for left back onto working needles. With WS facing, join yarn and work Row 2 of Chart A1 (A1, A1, A2, A2) across.

Work Rows 3–10 of Chart A1 (A1, A1, A2, A2).

Work Rows 1–10 of Chart A1 (A1, A1, A2, A2) once more.

Next row: *P1 (1, 1, 2, 2), k3, p2 (2, 2, 3, 3), k8, p2 (2, 2, 3, 3), k3, p2 (2, 2, 3, 3), k7, p1, rep from * once.

BO loosely.

right side

Sleeve

CO 58 (58, 58, 66, 66) sts, join for working in the round, being careful not to twist sts. Place marker to mark beg of round.

Set-up Round: *P1, k7, p2 (2, 2, 3, 3), k3, p2 (2, 2, 3, 3), k8, p2 (2, 2, 3, 3), k3, p1 (1, 1, 2, 2), rep from * once.

Work as for Left Sleeve, but follow Chart B1 (B1, B1, B2, B2) instead of Chart A1 or A2.

Shape Underarm

Work as for Left Sleeve, but follow Chart B1 (B1, B1, B2, B2) instead of Chart A1 or A2.

Upper Bodice

Work Row 1 as for Left Sleeve, but follow Chart B1 (B1, B1, B2, B2) instead of Chart A1 or A2.

Row 2: K1, p3, k2, p8, k2, p3, k2, p7, k1, work Row 2 of Chart B1 (B1, B1, B2, B2) twice, turn, CO 20 (20, 20, 22, 22) sts using backward loop cast-on, *do not* turn. Switch to longer circular needle if desired.

Work rest of Upper Bodice as for Left Side, but using Chart B1 (B1, B1, B2, B2) instead of Chart A1 or A2.

Shape Neck and Right Front

Row 1: Work Row 1 of Chart B1 (B1, B1, B2, B2).

Row 2: Work Row 2 of Chart B1 (B1, B1, B2, B2) twice, BO 5 (5, 5, 7, 7) sts, p1, k1, p3, k1, p2, k2 (2, 2, 3, 3), p3, k2 (2, 2, 3, 3), p7, k1, work Row 2 of Chart B1 (B1, B1, B2, B2).

Row 3: Work Row 3 of Chart B1 (B1, B1, B2, B2), p1 (1, 1, 2, 2), k1, k2tog, yo, k1, yo, ssk, k1, p2 (2, 2, 3, 3), 3-St Twist, p2 (2, 2, 3, 3), k2tog, yo2, ssk, k2tog, CO 2 sts using backwards-loop cast-on, ssk, p1, place next 58 (58, 58, 66, 66) sts on holder for right back.

Row 4: Skp, BO 3, p2, k1, p1, k2, p3, k2, p7, k1, work Row 4 of B1 (B1, B1, B2, B2).

Row 5: Work Row 5 of Chart B1 (B1, B1, B2, B2), p1, k2tog, yo, k3, yo, ssk, p2 (2, 2, 3, 3), k3, p2 (2, 2, 3, 3), k2tog, CO 2 sts using backwards loop, ssk, k1.

Row 6: Skp, BO 3 (3, 3, 4, 4), p1, k2, p3, k2 (2, 2, 3, 3), p7, work Row 6 of Chart B1 (B1, B1, B2, B2).

Row 7: Work Row 7 of Chart B1 (B1, B1, B2, B2), p1, k2tog, yo, k2, k2tog, yo, k1, p2 (2, 2, 3, 3), 3-St Twist, p2 (2, 2, 3, 3), k1.

Row 8: P1, k2 (2, 2, 3, 3), p3, k2 (2, 2, 3, 3), p7, k1, work Row 8 of Chart B1 (B1, B1, B2, B2).

Row 9: Work Row 9 of Chart B1 (B1, B1, B2, B2), p1, k2, yo, k3tog, yo, k2, p2 (2, 2, 3, 3), k3, p2 (2, 2, 3, 3), k1.

Row 10: Skp, k1 (1, 1, 2, 2), p3, k2 (2, 2, 3, 3), p7, k1, work Row 10 of Chart B1 (B1, B1, B2, B2).

Cut yarn, leaving tail for weaving in later. Place all sts on holder.

Right Back

Transfer 58 (58, 58, 66, 66) sts held for right back onto working needles. With RS facing, attach yarn and begin Row 3 of Chart B1 (B1, B1, B2, B2).

Work Rows 4-10 of Chart B1 (B1, B1, B2, B2).

Work Rows 1–10 of Chart B1 (B1, B1, B2, B2) once more.

Next row: *P1, k7, p2 (2, 2, 3, 3), k3, p2 (2, 2, 3, 3), k8, p2 (2, 2, 3, 3), k3, p1 (1, 1, 2, 2); rep from * once.

BO loosely.

assembling the upper bodice

Sew the side seam of the left front, sew the side seam of the right front. Sew the right back and left back together creating a seam at the center back.

body

With RS facing, pick up 122 (148, 174, 202, 228) sts around bottom edge of upper bodice.

Work in St st for 8½ (9, 9½, 10, 10)".

Change to smaller needles and work in k1, p1 rib for 1".

BO loosely in patt.

placket and collar

Using smaller needles, pick up and knit 36 (40, 42, 43, 43) sts along lower edge of right front of cardigan; k 44 (44, 44, 49, 49) sts from holder for right front; pick up and knit 18 (18, 18, 20, 20) sts along right neckline, 26 sts along back of neck, and 18 (18, 18, 20, 20) sts along left neckline; k 44 (44, 44, 49, 49) sts from holder for left front; and finally, pick up and knit 36 (40, 42, 43, 43) sts along lower edge of left front of cardigan.

Work in k1, p1 rib for 2½".

BO loosely in patt.

finishing

Block sweater as desired. Weave in all ends.

SANTORINI

linen kimono jacket

by Lisa Limber

Nothing says summer like linen! This kimono-style jacket, knit in crisp linen, will quickly become a warm-weather favorite. Santorini's well-planned proportions and straightforward construction mean it's easy to wear and goes with everything, whether it's a sundress or your favorite shorts and tank top. In cooler weather, try it over a blouse or long-sleeved tee.

pattern notes

Marking each bind-off row with a locking-ring marker will make it easy to keep track of how many stitches you've bound off.

The Wavy Lace Chart is an 8-row pattern; yarn overs and decreases are worked on RS *and* WS rows.

Bind off loosely for the cuffs, using a larger needle size if necessary, to create an undulating edge. For the neckband, however, bind off normally to maintain a smooth line.

The charts used in this pattern are available for you to download and print at **www.wiley.com/go/knittinginthesun**.

directions

back

Border

Using the cable cast-on method, CO 88 (98, 108, 118, 128) sts.

Knit 5 rows to create garter-st edging.

Next row (WS): K4, place marker (pm), *k10, pm, rep from * to last 4 sts, k4.

Follow the Wavy Lace Chart, beginning with Row 1 (a RS row), for next 8 rows, knitting the first and last 4 sts of all rows.

Knit 5 more rows ending with a WS row.

SIZE
S (M, L, 1X, 2X)

FINISHED MEASUREMENTS
Chest circumference: 40 (44, 48, 52, 56)"
Length: 20 (22, 24, 26, 28)"

MATERIALS
- Louet *Euroflax* (100% linen; 270 yd. per 100g skein); color: 35 Mustard; 4 (5, 6, 7, 8) skeins
- US 7 (4.5mm) circular needle, 24" or longer (*or size needed to match gauge*)
- Locking-ring stitch markers
- 4 stitch holders
- Tapestry needle

GAUGE
18 sts × 23 rows = 4" in St st, blocked

SKILLS USED
increasing, decreasing, picking up stitches, three-needle bind-off, basic lace knitting

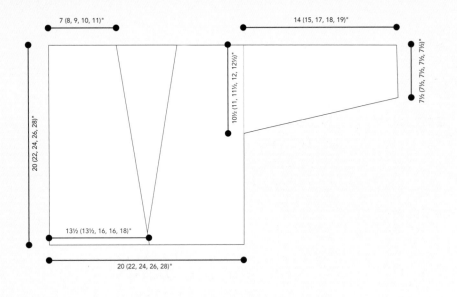

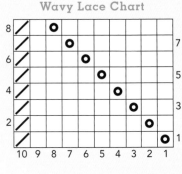

Wavy Lace Chart

Key to Wavy Lace Chart

knit
K on RS, P on WS

yo
yarn over

k2tog
RS: Knit 2 sts together as 1 st
WS: Purl 2 sts together as 1 st

Body

Continue in St st for 17½ (19½, 21½, 23½, 25½)" (not including lace border), ending with a RS row.

Next row (WS): K33 (37, 41, 45, 49) sts, then place them on a holder for right shoulder, BO center 22 (24, 26, 28, 30) sts for back neck, k33 (37, 41, 45, 49) sts and place them on second st holder for left shoulder. Finished length is approximately 20 (22, 24, 26, 28)".

left front

Border

Using cable cast-on method, CO 48 (48, 58, 58, 68) sts.

Knit 5 rows to create garter-st edging.

Next row (WS): K4, pm, *k10, pm, rep from * to last 4 sts, k4.

Follow the Wavy Lace Chart for next 8 rows, knitting the first and last 4 sts of all rows.

Knit 5 more rows ending with a WS row.

Body

The rest of the front is worked in St st.

Begin shaping the kimono front as follows:

Next row (Dec Row) (RS): K to last 3 sts, k2tog, k1.

Rep Dec Row every 6th (10th, 6th, 10th, 6th) row 14 (10, 16, 12, 17) more times. 33 (37, 41, 45, 49) sts rem. Work even until piece measures 20 (22, 24, 26, 28)".

Do not BO. Join sts to sts held for left shoulder of back using the three-needle bind-off (see "Special Knitting Techniques" appendix).

right front

CO and knit the Border as for Left Front.

Body

The rest of the front is worked in St st.

Begin shaping the kimono front as follows:

Next row (Dec Row) (RS): K1, ssk, k to end of row.

Rep Dec Row every 6th (10th, 6th, 10th, 6th) row 14 (10, 16, 12, 17) more times. 33 (37, 41, 45, 49) sts rem. Work even until this piece measures 20 (22, 24, 26, 28)".

Do not BO. Join sts to sts held for right shoulder of back using the three-needle bind-off.

sleeves

(make 2)

Measure 10½ (11, 11½, 12, 12½)" from shoulder seam on front and pm. Rep on back of garment.

With RS facing, pick up 96 (100, 104, 108, 112) sts between the 2 markers. Be sure to pick up the same number of sts on both sides of shoulder seam.

Work 3 rows in St st.

Next row (Dec row) (RS): K1, ssk, k to last 3 sts, k2tog, k1.

Continue in St st and rep Dec Row every 4th row 13 (15, 17, 19, 21) more times. 68 sts (for all sizes).

Work even until sleeve measures 11 (12, 14, 15, 16)", or 3" shorter than desired length, ending with a WS row.

Border

Knit 3 rows.

Next row (WS): K4, pm, *k10, pm, rep from * to last 4 sts, k4.

Follow the Wavy Lace Chart for next 8 rows, knitting first and last 4 sts of all rows.

Knit 5 more rows ending with a RS row.

BO loosely on the WS.

neckband

With RS facing, begin just above the Wavy Lace border on right front and pick up and knit 218 (238, 268, 288, 318) sts evenly up right front, around back neck, and down left front, ending at the top of Wavy Lace border on left front.

Knit 2 rows.

Next row (WS): K4, pm, *k10, pm, rep from * to last 4 sts, k4.

Follow the Wavy Lace Chart for next 8 rows, beginning with Row 1 (a RS row), knitting first and last 4 sts of all rows.

Knit 3 rows ending on a RS row.

BO firmly on WS.

finishing

Block cardigan before seaming. Use steam, if desired, to flatten seams and lace. Sew underarm and side seams. Weave in ends.

ODDS & ENDS

BLACK SEA

gored skirt

by Faina Goberstein

Inspired by a combination of comfort and style suitable for a warm climate, this elegant skirt is suitable for any occasion. Its silhouette is becoming for most figure types. The skirt is knit in the round in reverse stockinette with six strategically placed triangles around the bottom. Continuous lines from the tops of triangles give an illusion of six panels. Twirl and you can see those triangles dance!

pattern notes

This skirt is designed for a close fit. Choose the size that most closely matches your hip measurement. Elastic at the waist will ensure a perfect fit.

The Black Sea skirt features reverse stockinette stitch and is worked in the round. Because most knitters find it easier to knit than to purl, the pattern is written "inside out." Keep your tails on the knit side of the work and simply turn the piece right side out at the end.

directions

skirt body

Using largest needles (US 9, or size needed to match gauge), CO 192 (216, 228, 252, 264, 288, 300) sts. Place marker (pm) and join to work in the round, being careful not to twist sts.

Rounds 1–5 (WS): *P1, [k3, p1] twice, [k1, p1] 7 (9, 10, 12, 13, 15, 16) times, k1, [p1, k3] twice; rep from * to end.

Rounds 6–28: *P1, [k3, p1] twice, k15 (19, 21, 25, 27, 31, 33), [p1, k3] twice; rep from * to end.

Change to needles one size smaller (US 8 or size needed to match gauge).

SIZE
XS (S, M, L, 1X, 2X, 3X)

FINISHED MEASUREMENTS
Waist circumference (excluding elastic): 28 (33, 36, 40½, 43, 47, 50)"

Hip circumference: 32 (37, 40, 45, 48, 53, 56)"

Length: 27 (28, 28½, 29, 29½, 30, 30½)"

MATERIALS
- Berroco *Linen Jeans* (70% rayon, 30% linen; 80 yd. per 50g skein); color: 7405 New Khaki; 10 (12, 14, 16, 17, 18, 19) skeins
- US 9 (5.5mm) circular needle, 24" or 29" length (*or size needed to match gauge*)
- US 8 (5mm) circular needle, 24" or 29" length
- US 7 (4.5mm) circular needle, 24" or 29" length
- US 6 (4mm) circular needle, 24" or 29" length
- 1 to 2 yd. of 1"-wide elastic for waistband

continued ➤

➤ continued

- Stitch marker
- Tapestry needle
- Sewing needle
- Thread

GAUGE

16 sts × 25 rows = 4" in St st on US 9 needles

17 sts × 26 rows = 4" in St st on US 8 needles

18 sts × 27 rows = 4" in St st on US 7 needles

20 sts × 28 rows = 4" in St st on US 6 needles

SKILLS USED

decreasing, knitting in the round

Round 29 (Dec Round): *P1, [k1, k2tog, p1] twice, k15 (19, 21, 25, 27, 31, 33), [p1, k2tog, k1] twice; rep from * to end. 168 (192, 204, 228, 240, 264, 276) sts.

Rounds 30–50: *P1, [k2, p1] twice, k15 (19, 21, 25, 27, 31, 33), [p1, k2] twice; rep from * to end.

Round 51 (Dec Round): *P1, [k2tog, p1] twice, k15 (19, 21, 25, 27, 31, 33), [p1, k2tog] twice; rep from * to end. 144 (168, 180, 204, 216, 240, 252) sts.

Rounds 52–76: *P1, [k1, p1] twice, k15 (19, 21, 25, 27, 31, 33), [p1, k1] twice; rep from * to end.

Rounds 77–95: *P1, k1, p1, k19 (23, 25, 29, 31, 35, 37), p1, k1; rep from * to end.

Round 96: *P1, k23 (27, 29, 33, 35, 39, 41); rep from * to end.

Change to needles one size smaller (US 7 or size needed to match gauge).

Rep Round 96 until skirt measures 24 (25, 25½, 26, 26½, 27, 27½)" from cast-on edge.

Change to needles one size smaller (US 6 or size needed to match gauge).

Work Round 96 ten more times.

waistband

Beg working in rib as follows:

Next round: *P1, k1; rep from * to end.

Rep this round 9 more times.

Knit 1 round to form turning ridge.

Purl 9 rounds.

BO all sts purlwise.

finishing

Turn the skirt purl-side out.

Weave in all ends on the knit side. Block the skirt, using light steam, and straighten the lines that form triangles. Allow skirt to dry.

Cut elastic approximately 1½" less than actual waist measurement.

Fold waistband along the turning round to the inside of the skirt and sew the bound-off edge to beg of ribbed waistband, leaving a 2" opening. Attach a large safety pin to one end of elastic and draw it through waistband. Double-check the fit, then secure ends of elastic together. Stitch final 2" of waistband closed and re-block waistband as needed.

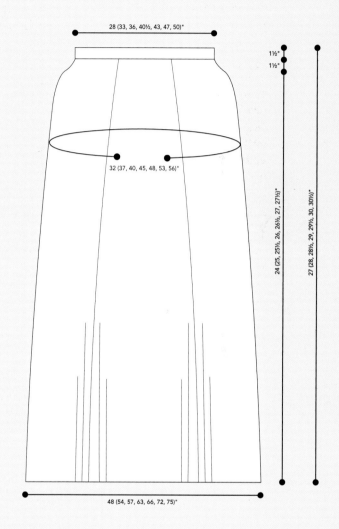

28 (33, 36, 40½, 43, 47, 50)"

1½"
1½"

32 (37, 40, 45, 48, 53, 56)"

24 (25, 25½, 26, 26½, 27, 27½)"

27 (28, 28½, 29, 29½, 30, 30½)"

48 (54, 57, 63, 66, 72, 75)"

CABRILLO
openwork skirt

by Kristi Porter

I love to wear skirts in warm weather. This one, with a biased fishnet pattern, has great movement and a breezy quality that make it perfect for a night out in a seaside town. The nubby blend of silk, linen, and synthetics in this yarn is earthy, but with a hint of sparkle—a perfect choice for this easy-to-work skirt. Wear it over leggings, a slip, or a simple straight skirt to vary the look.

pattern notes

Choose the size that most closely matches your hip size; elastic at the waist will ensure a perfect fit.

Make sure your marker doesn't migrate into the yarn overs as you work around.

three-needle join

Hold 2 needles parallel in left hand, *insert RH needle into first st on front needle and first st on back needle; k these 2 sts together; rep from * around.

directions
waistband

CO 96 (108, 120, 132, 144, 156, 168) sts using provisional cast-on (see "Special Knitting Techniques" appendix). Place marker (pm) and join in the round, being careful not to twist sts.

Knit 10 rounds.

Purl 1 round to form turning ridge.

Knit 10 rounds.

SIZE
XS (S, M, L, 1X, 2X, 3X)

FINISHED MEASUREMENTS
Hip circumference: 32 (36, 40, 44, 48, 52, 56)"

Length: 30 (30, 31, 31, 32, 32, 32)"

MATERIALS
- Berroco *Seduce* (47% rayon, 25% linen, 17% silk, 11% nylon; 100 yd. per 40g skein); color: 4448 Verdigris; 5 (5, 6, 7, 7, 8, 9) skeins
- US 10 (6mm) circular needle, 24" or 36" length (*or size needed to match gauge*)
- Spare circular needle
- 1 to 2 yd. of ½" elastic
- Stitch holder
- Stitch marker
- Tapestry needle
- Sewing needle
- Thread

continued ➤

➤ continued

GAUGE

12 sts × 14 rows = 4" over fishnet pattern of skirt, unblocked, lightly stretched

14 sts × 26 rows = 4" over St st, unblocked

SKILLS USED

increasing, decreasing, provisional cast-on, knitting in the round, three-needle join, grafting (Kitchener stitch)

Transfer sts from provisional cast-on to second circular needle. Fold work on the purl ridge and join sts from both needles together using the three-needle join. Continue to 10 sts before marker. Slip these 10 sts from provisional cast-on to holder to create an opening to insert the elastic later; knit 10 rem sts. 96 (108, 120, 132, 144, 156, 168) sts on needle.

body of skirt

Round 1: *Yo2, k2tog; rep from * around.

Round 2: Knit, letting extra wraps fall. 96 (108, 120, 132, 144, 156, 168) sts.

Rep these 2 rows until skirt measures 28 (28, 29, 29, 30, 30, 30)", or 2" short of desired length.

Next round: *Yo2, k2tog; rep from * around.

Next round: Knit, but work 2 sts (k1, p1) into each double yo. 144 (162, 180, 198, 216, 234, 252) sts.

bottom border

Knit 10 rounds.

Purl 1 round to form turning ridge.

Knit 9 rounds.

BO very loosely, using larger needle if necessary.

finishing

Block skirt by soaking in cool water then lying flat to dry.

Sew bound-off edge to beg of bottom border.

Cut elastic to your waist measurement plus 2". Thread elastic through casing. Double-check the fit, overlap the elastic and sew ends together securely. Graft sts (see "Special Knitting Techniques" appendix) from holder to opposite side of casing, concealing the elastic.

Weave in remaining ends.

16 (18, 20, 22, 24, 26)"

30 (30, 31, 31, 32, 32, 32)"

COPACABANA
bathing suit

COPACABANA
bathing suit

by Tonya Wagner

This March, when we were enduring near-freezing temperatures in Kentucky, my husband's job as a jazz guitarist took him to Brazil. I couldn't help but feel jealous that he was enjoying eighty-degree weather in a beautiful country. His trip did, however, motivate me to start thinking about the warm weather that was just around the corner.

These boy short–style bottoms are knit from the top down in one piece. Ribbing at the leg openings helps them to stay in place. The bandeau top has a retro feel with convertible straps that you can wear crisscrossed in front or back, or as a halter. Optional short-row shaping allows buxom knitters to create a custom fit. Both pieces feature encased elastic, which, paired with a stretchy cotton-lycra yarn, gives you a swimsuit that stays in place whether you're lounging by the pool or going for a dip in the sea.

pattern notes

This pattern contains a lot of negative ease so the finished pieces may look small. They will stretch quite a bit and should fit you snugly, but not tightly. The yarn you use is crucial to the fit of the garment. Do not substitute a yarn that has no elasticity.

To get a custom fit, choose the top and bottom sizes that are right for you. This may mean knitting a medium bottom and a small top. Curvaceous women will want to incorporate the optional short-row bust shaping to make a bandeau top that is larger in the front without being larger everywhere else. Measure your chest above the bust to determine which size to knit and follow the short-row shaping appropriate for your cup size.

SIZE
XS (S, M, L, 1X)

FINISHED MEASUREMENTS
Chest circumference:
24 (27, 30½, 33¾, 37)", unstretched

Fits chest circumference up to:
30 (34, 38, 42, 46)"

Low-waist circumference:
16 (20, 24, 28, 32)", unstretched

Fits hip circumference up to:
32 (36, 40, 44, 48)"

MATERIALS
- Cascade Yarns *Fixation* (98.3% cotton, 1.7% lycra; 100 yd. per 50g skein); color: 7382 Brown; 2 (3, 3, 3, 3) skeins for bottom; 3 (3, 4, 4, 5) skeins for top

continued ➤

➤ **continued**

- US 5 (3.75mm) circular needle, 24" length (*or size needed to match gauge*)
- US 5 (3.75mm) circular needle, 16" length
- US 3 (3.25mm) circular needle, 16" length
- 2 stitch markers, in contrasting colors
- Tapestry needle
- 2 yd. of ¼" swimsuit elastic
- 4 buttons, ¾" diameter
- Sewing needle
- Thread

GAUGE
24 sts × 40 rows = 4" in St st with larger needles

SKILLS USED
short-row shaping, knitting in the round, increasing, basic sewing

directions
bottom

With 24" circular needle, CO 96 (120, 144, 168, 192) sts.

Working back and forth, work in garter st for 1".

Join in the round, being careful not to twist sts. Place marker (pm) to indicate beg of round. This marks the center back.

K48 (60, 72, 84, 96) sts, place contrasting marker to indicate center front, k to end of round.

Begin inc as follows:

> Round 1: Knit.
>
> Round 2: Knit.
>
> Round 3: Kfb, k to 1 st before marker, kfb, slip marker (sm), kfb, k to 1 st before marker, kfb. 4 sts increased.

Rep these 3 rounds 10 (15, 18, 24, 26) more times.

Rep Rounds 2 and 3 only 8 (6, 5, 0, 0) times.

Rep Round 3 only 2 (0, 0, 0, 0) times. 180 (208, 240, 268, 300) sts.

Legs
Switch to larger 16" circular needle and knit to first marker. (You will work the first leg on these sts only.) Hold rem 90 (104, 120, 134, 150) sts on 24" circular needle for second leg.

Using backward loop or knitted cast-on, CO 11 (12, 12, 11, 11) sts, pm, CO 11 (12, 12, 11, 11) sts, and join in the round being careful not to twist sts. 112 (128, 144, 156, 172) sts.

Work in St st for 1 (1, 1¼, 1½, 2)", or to desired length.

Change to smaller 16" circular needle and work 6 rows in k2, p2 rib.

BO loosely in patt.

Transfer held sts to larger 16" circular needle and work second leg the same as the first.

bandeau top

With 24" circular needle, CO 144 (162, 182, 202, 222) sts.

Working back and forth, work in garter st for 1".

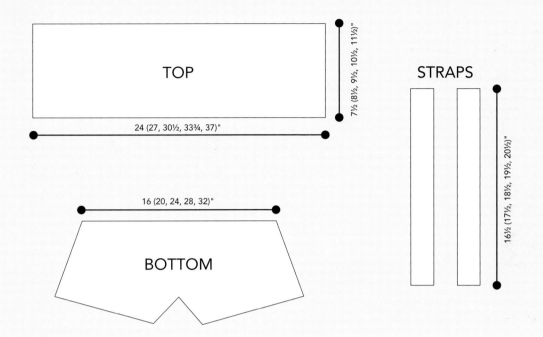

TOP

7½ (8½, 9½, 10½, 11½)"

24 (27, 30½, 33¾, 37)"

STRAPS

16½ (17½, 18½, 19½, 20½)"

16 (20, 24, 28, 32)"

BOTTOM

Join in the round, being careful not to twist sts. Place marker to indicate beg of round. K72 (81, 91, 101, 111), place contrasting marker, and k to end of round.

Work 6 rounds in St st.

Optional Short-row Shaping

For a larger bust, short-row shaping will add more coverage in the front. For C (D, DD) cup sizes, follow these directions. You will work back and forth over the short-row section.

Row 1 (RS): K to 3 sts before marker, w&t.

Row 2 (WS): P to 3 sts before contrasting marker, w&t.

Row 3: K to 4 sts before marker, w&t.

Row 4: P to 4 sts before contrasting marker, w&t.

Continue short rows as established, until you are wrapping and turning 6 (9, 12) sts before markers.

Next row (RS): K across, picking up wraps and knitting them together with sts they wrap.

All Sizes Continue

Continue knitting in the round in St st until top measures 5½ (6½, 7½, 8½, 9½)" from cast-on edge. If you've added short rows, make sure you measure up the back, outside the short-row shaping.

Work in garter st for 1".

BO loosely.

straps

(make 2)

With larger 16" circular needle, CO 7 sts.

Knit 3 rows.

Create Buttonholes

Row 1: K2, BO 3, k2.

Row 2: K2, CO 3 sts using backward-loop cast-on, k2.

Work in garter st for 16 (17, 18, 19, 20)" or desired length. Depending on your proportions and how you want to wear your straps, you may wish to shorten or lengthen the straps.

Rep Rows 1 and 2.

Knit 3 rows.

BO.

finishing

Weave in all ends.

bottom

Cut swimsuit elastic 1" shorter than casing. With WS facing and using a sewing needle and thread, tack one end of elastic to garter-st casing so it sits just above St st fabric. Stretch elastic to other side and tack into place. Fold casing to the inside and sew into place using yarn or thread.

bandeau top

On cast-on edge, attach elastic and work casing as for Bottom.

Sew 2 buttons to front of swimsuit top at bound-off edge, centered and 7 (8, 9, 10, 11) " apart. Sew 2 buttons on back the same way. Attach straps as desired.

VERNAZZA
summer sleep set

VERNAZZA

summer sleep set

by Julia Trice

O h, those summer nights! When things get hot, you want to stay cool but still look great. Slip into this sleep set that you knit in comfortable cotton and bamboo, and you can lounge in style. And the camisole, with its subtle bust shaping, gently gathered empire waist, and lace details, is ready to wear on it's own or under a light jacket during the daytime, too.

pattern notes

For the camisole, choose a size slightly smaller than your actual bust measurement. If you are at the smaller end of a size range, consider using US 3 (3mm) circular needle for the bust section only to ensure a good fit.

For the tap pants, take your measurements at the largest part of your posterior, and choose a size that gives you at least 1" of ease in that area.

The charts used in this pattern are available for you to download and print at **www.wiley.com/go/knittinginthesun**.

directions

CAMISOLE

You work the camisole flat in two pieces from hem to bust; then you join the pieces and work the bust in the round.

back bodice

Using larger circular needle, CO 94 (103, 121, 130, 139) sts using long-tail cast-on method. Beginning with WS row, follow the Vine Lace Chart for 6 rows.

SIZE
XS (S, M, L, 1X)

FINISHED MEASUREMENTS

CAMISOLE

Chest circumference: 27½ (31½, 35, 39, 42½)"

Hemline circumference: 37½ (40¾, 46, 49½, 53)"

Length (excluding straps): 18¾ (19¾, 20¾, 21¾, 22¾)"

TAP PANTS

Leg circumference: 24 (27½, 30½, 34½, 36)"

Waist circumference: 26½ (30½, 34½, 38½, 42½)"

To fit hip circumferences up to: 35 (39, 43, 47, 51)"

Length: 11¼ (12, 12¾, 13, 14¼)"

continued ➤

Sizes S, M, and 1X Only

Row 7: Purl to last 3 sts, p2tog, p1.

Sizes XS and L Only

Row 7: Purl.

94 (102, 120, 130, 138) sts.

Work 2 rows even in St st.

Next row (Dec Row) (RS): K29 (32, 37, 40, 43), ssk, place marker (pm), k32 (34, 42, 46, 48), pm, k2tog, k29 (32, 37, 40, 43).

Dec every 14 (20, 10, 12, 14) rows 4 (3, 7, 6, 5) more times as follows:

> K to 2 sts before first marker, ssk, slip marker (sm), k to next marker, sm, k2tog, k to end. 84 (94, 104, 116, 126) sts.

Work 6 rows even in St st, or until piece measures 10¾ (11¼, 11¾, 12¼, 12¾)" from cast-on edge.

Gathers

Next RS row: K34 (39, 44, 50, 55), pm, work Row 1 of Bodice Gathers Chart over next 16 sts, pm, k to end of row.

Work next 5 rows in St st, continuing to follow Bodice Gathers Chart between markers.

Work 1 row in St st.

Braids

Next row (WS): "Purl under" by wrapping yarn clockwise under needle.

Next row (RS): Kfb, *slip closest st on RH needle back to LH needle without twisting it; go behind first st on LH needle, k through back loop of second st, leaving st on needle; k first st on LH needle through back loop and slide both sts off LH needle; rep from * across row.

Rep these 2 rows once more.

Work 1 row in St st.

Put 72 (82, 92, 102, 112) sts onto spare circular needle or scrap yarn to hold.

➤ continued

MATERIALS

- Classic Elite *Cotton Bam Boo* (52% cotton, 48% bamboo; 130 yd. per 50g ball); color: 3635 Willow; 6 (6, 7, 8, 9) balls for camisole; 3 (4, 5, 6, 6) balls for tap pants
- US 5 (3.75mm) circular needle, 24" length (*or size needed to match gauge*)
- US 3 (3.25mm) circular needle, 24" length
- US 3 (3.25mm) double-pointed needles (for camisole only)
- Spare circular needle or scrap yarn
- 3½ yd. of ½" elastic (makes camisole and tap pants)
- 2 stitch markers in contrasting colors
- Safety pin for camisole straps
- Tapestry needle
- Sewing needle
- Thread

GAUGE

21 sts × 32 rows = 4" in St st, blocked

SKILLS USED

increasing, decreasing, knitting from charts, short-row shaping, I-cord

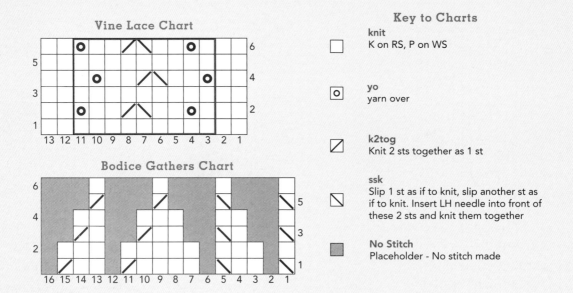

Vine Lace Chart

Bodice Gathers Chart

Key to Charts

knit
K on RS, P on WS

yo
yarn over

k2tog
Knit 2 sts together as 1 st

ssk
Slip 1 st as if to knit, slip another st as if to knit. Insert LH needle into front of these 2 sts and knit them together

No Stitch
Placeholder - No stitch made

front bodice

Using larger circular needle, CO 103 (112, 121, 130, 139) sts using long-tail cast-on method. Beg with WS row, follow Vine Lace Chart for 6 rows.

Sizes S, M, and 1X Only

Row 7: Purl to last 3 sts, p2tog, p1.

Sizes XS and L Only

Row 7: Purl.

102 (112, 120, 130, 138) sts.

Work 2 rows even in St st.

Next row (Dec Row) (RS): K24 (27, 29, 32, 34), ssk, pm, k50 (54, 58, 62, 66), pm, k2tog, k24 (27, 29, 32, 34).

Dec every 8 (8, 12, 12, 14) rows 8 (8, 6, 6, 5) more times as follows:

K to 2 sts before first marker, ssk, sm, k to next marker, sm, k2tog, k to end. 84 (94, 106, 116, 126) sts.

Work 6 rows even in St st.

Work Gathers and Braids sections as for Back Bodice. 72 (82, 92, 102, 112) sts.

Bust

Transfer sts held for Back Bodice onto circular needle with Front Bodice sts, making sure that both right sides face outward and Front Bodice is first on LH needle when you beg to work. 144 (164, 184, 204, 224) sts.

Join to work in the round and pm to mark left side seam, work across front and place contrasting marker to mark right side seam.

Work even in St st until the piece measures 3 (3½, 4, 4, 4)" (or to fullest point of your bust, with Braid section below your bust, even with band of your bra), then use short rows to shape the bust as follows:

> *Row 1: From beg of round marker, k58 (66, 74, 82, 90), sl next st onto RH needle, wrap yarn to WS and turn work.*
>
> *Row 2: Working flat, sl first st to RH needle, p44 (50, 56, 62, 68), sl next st onto RH needle, wrap yarn to RS and turn work.*
>
> *Row 3: Sl first st to RH needle, k to wrapped st, k wrap together with st it wraps, k1, sl next st onto RH needle, wrap yarn to WS and turn work.*
>
> *Row 4: Sl first st to RH needle, p to wrapped st, purl wrap together with st it wraps, p1, sl next st onto RH needle, wrap yarn to RS and turn work.*

For cup sizes A (B, C, D), rep Rows 3 and 4 0 (1, 2, 3) more times. Depending on your cup size, you may need to work past side markers. Do so and then replace them.

Next row: Sl first st to RH needle and resume working in the round, picking up wraps you encounter and knitting them together with sts they wrap.

When Front measures 6½ (7, 7½, 8, 8½)", or the camisole fits as you wish, create the picot turning edge as follows:

Next round: *Yo, k2tog; rep from * to end.

Change to smaller circular needle and k 10 rounds to create casing for the elastic. Do not BO.

straps (optional)

Using dpns, k a 2-st I-cord 40" to 45" long. Do not BO. Place live sts on a safety pin so that you can easily shorten or lengthen cord for optimal fit later. Secure ends together temporarily with the safety pin.

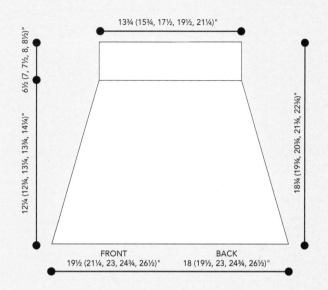

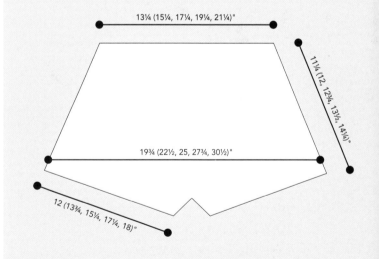

finishing

Cut a piece of elastic about 1" longer than the bust circumference of camisole. Overlap ends of elastic by ½" and sew together.

Turn camisole inside out, keeping sts on needles.

Turn top edge of camisole down, folding work over at picot edging. Place elastic inside the fold.

If you are making straps, remove safety pin from cast-on end of cord. Thread I-cord through eyelets as follows:

> *Beginning on left front, pull I-cord through 10th (11th, 12th, 13th, 15th) eyelet from marker from WS to RS, go down through 12th (13th, 15th, 17th, 18th) eyelet from marker on right back from RS to WS, bring I-cord along the back through casing, then up through 12th (13th, 15th, 17th, 18th) eyelet from opposite marker on back from WS to RS, then bring I-cord down through 10th (11th, 12th, 13th, 15th) eyelet from marker on right front. The straps are straight in front and crossed in back. Pin ends of strap together.*

Using a tapestry needle, sew live sts down to main body, securing elastic and cording inside. Slip each live st off needle as you go. Leave a small opening and make sure the section of I-cord with safety pin remains visible.

Using a tapestry needle, sew up side seams of camisole. Try camisole on and adjust the straps, shortening or lengthening them as needed. When they are the desired length, sew ends together and conceal the join under the casing.

Weave in ends. Wash and block according to yarn instructions.

TAP PANTS

You work the tap pants in the round from the bottom up.

legs

Using larger circular needle, CO 126 (144, 162, 180, 198) sts using long-tail cast-on method. Place marker (pm) and join to work in the round, being careful not to twist sts.

Beg working Vine Lace Chart, but use 9-st rep within the red box only (you do not use the 2 edge sts on each side when working this patt in the round). Work all 6 rounds of Vine Lace Chart.

Work 12 rounds even in St st.

Next round: K to last 5 (6, 7, 8, 9) sts, BO 5 (6, 7, 8, 9) sts, remove marker, BO 5 (6, 7, 8, 9) sts of following round, knit to last 2 sts in round, k2tog. 115 (131, 147, 163, 179) sts.

Turn work and beg working flat in St st.

Row 1: BO 3 (4, 5, 6, 7) sts, p to last 2 sts, p2tog.

Row 2: BO 3 (4, 5, 6, 7) sts, k to last 2 sts, k2tog.

Row 3: P2tog-tbl, p to last 2 sts, p2tog.

Row 4: K to last 2 sts, k2tog. 104 (118, 132, 146, 160) sts.

Transfer sts to spare needle or scrap yarn.

Make second leg the same, but leave it on the needle with working yarn still attached.

Transfer sts held for first leg back onto circular needle with second leg, so that right sides are out and bound-off sections of each leg face one another in center of circular needle. 208 (236, 264, 292, 320) sts.

body

Place marker and beg to work in the round. The points where bound-off edges meet mark center front and center back of tap pants. Knit to second join, place contrasting stitch marker.

Next round (Dec Round): K to last st in round, *sl last st, remove marker, k2tog, psso, pm just before last st on RH needle,* k to 1 st before contrasting marker and rep from * to *. 4 sts decreased.

Continue in St st and rep Dec Round every 3rd round, 16 (18, 20, 22, 24) more times. 140 (160, 180, 200, 220) sts.

Knit 15 rounds even.

waistband

Next round: *Yo, k2tog; rep from * to end to form picot turning ridge.

Change to smaller circular needle and k 10 rounds even. Do not BO.

finishing

Cut a piece of elastic about 1" longer than waist circumference of tap pants. Overlap ends of elastic by ½" and sew together.

Turn tap pants inside out, keeping live sts on needles.

Turn waistband down at picot turning ridge. Place elastic inside the fold. Using a tapestry needle, sew live sts down to main body, securing elastic inside. Sl each st off needles as you go.

Seam up bound-off edges of the crotch.

Weave in ends. Wash and block according to yarn instructions.

HALEAKALA

beach chair

by Heather Broadhurst

A trip to the beach or a concert in the park often means bringing your own chair. Why not do it in style? This pattern allows you to re-create your drugstore-variety folding chair into a handknit beauty.

pattern notes

If your chair still has its back and seat attached, use them as templates for this pattern.

When working flat, work a selvedge stitch on every row by slipping the first stitch purlwise.

applied I-cord

With RS facing, CO 4 sts, and place on a dpn. *K3, sl 1 st knitwise, k1 from selvedge edge, pass the sl st over the st just knit, do not turn, slide sts to opposite end of needle and rep from * until all selvedge edge sts are consumed.

directions

NOTE The chair back begins as a center-out circle and then becomes an octagonal sunburst. You then use short-row shaping to change the octagon into a square that is then knit outward to form a rectangle. You will pick up stitches from a slipped-stitch row and work those stitches together with the live stitches from each side of the rectangle in a three-needle bind-off to attach the back to the chair frame.

FINISHED MEASUREMENTS
Back: 15" × 18", or to fit your chair
Seat: 13" × 18"

MATERIALS
- J & P Coats *Crochet Nylon* (100% nylon; 150 yd. per spool); color 43 beige; 7 spools
- US 5 (3.75mm) double-pointed needles *(or size needed to match gauge)*
- US 5 (3.75mm) straight needles
- 2 sets of US 5 (3.75mm) circular needles, any length
- Aluminum-frame beach chair
- Tapestry needle
- Stitch holders or scrap yarn
- Non-porous household glue

GAUGE
20 sts × 24 rows = 4" in St st

SKILLS USED
increasing, decreasing, applied I-cord, short-row shaping, double-pointed needles, three-needle bind-off, unconventional construction

chair back

Using dpns, CO 8 sts and divide evenly among 4 needles, join, being careful not to twist the sts, and knit with a fifth needle. When there are too many stitches to fit comfortably on the dpns, switch to the circular needle.

Round 1: [K1, yo] 8 times. 16 sts.

Rounds 2, 4, 6, 8, and 10: Knit.

Round 3: [K1, yo] 16 times. 32 sts.

Round 5: [K1, yo] 32 times. 64 sts.

Rounds 7, 9, and 11: [K2tog, yo] 32 times.

Round 12: [K2, yo] 32 times. 96 sts.

Rounds 13 and 15: Knit.

Rounds 14 and 16: [K2tog, yo] 48 times.

Round 17: [K3, yo] 32 times. 128 sts.

Rounds 18: Knit.

Round 19: *K1, [k2tog, yo] 7 times, k1, rep from * around.

Rounds 20, 22, 24, and 26: Knit.

Round 21: *K2, [k2tog, yo] 6 times, k2, rep from * around.

Round 23: *K1, M1L, k2, [k2tog, yo] 5 times, k2, M1R, k1, rep from * around. 144 sts.

Round 25: *K5, [k2tog, yo] 4 times, k5, rep from * around.

Round 27: *K6, [k2tog, yo] 3 times, k6 rep from * around.

Round 28: *K1, M1L, k16, M1R, k1, rep from * around. 160 sts.

Round 29: *K8, [k2tog, yo] twice, k8, rep from * around.

Rounds 30 and 32: Knit.

Round 31: *K9, k2tog, yo, k9, rep from * around.

Round 33: *K1, M1L, k18, M1R, k1, rep from * around. 176 sts.

Rounds 34–37: Knit.

Round 38: *K1, M1L, k20, M1R, k1, rep from * around. 192 sts (24 sts on each side of the octagon).

Rounds 39 and 40: Knit.

begin short-row shaping

The octagon and sunburst are now complete. You will now use short-row shaping on 4 of the 8 wedges to form a square.

NOTE In these short-row segments, simply turn the work, do not wrap. Slip the first stitch of every odd row purlwise.

***Row 1 (RS): Sl 1, k1, turn.

Row 2 and all WS rows: Purl.

Row 3: Sl 1p, k3, turn.

Odd rows 5–21: Continue as established, slipping the first st as if to purl and knitting 2 additional sts on each RS row until 22 sts of the first octagon segment are consumed.

Row 23: Sl 1, k47.

Turn work and on WS, join new yarn to work short rows on the third octagon segment.

Row 1 (WS): Sl 1, p1, turn.

Row 2 and all RS rows: Knit.

Row 3: Sl 1, p3, turn.

Odd rows 5–21: Continue as established, slipping the first st as if to purl and purling 2 additional sts on each WS row.

Row 23: Sl 1, p23.

Cut yarn leaving an 8" tail and tie a knot about 1" from the end of yarn to prevent fraying.

With yarn from the first octagon segment, k24, turn work.

Next row (WS): Sl 1, p71.

Next row (RS): *Sl 1, k1, rep from * across these 72 sts.

Work in St st until piece measures 5", or length required by your chair frame, from this slipped st row. Place 72 sts on holder.

Rep from *** on the opposite side of the octagon.

pick up to form tube

With WS facing, join new yarn and pick up and knit 36 sts from the slipped st row.

Next row: Kfb across. Leave these 72 sts on the needle.

Rep for other side.

optional top tab

This tab will help to keep the chair back in place.

With WS facing, join new yarn to the 24 live sts at the top of the back, p24.

Next row (RS): *Sl 1, k1, rep from * across.

Work in St st until work measures 5" from this slipped st row.

With WS facing, on a second needle, join new yarn and pick up and knit 12 sts from the slipped st row.

Next row: Kfb all sts and leave these 24 sts on the needle.

finishing

Finish the top edge with applied I-cord as follows: Pick up 30 sts across the top of the knitted back by running a needle through the selvedge

sts. Work applied I-cord (see "Pattern Notes") on these sts. If you do not work the optional top tab, when you reach the 24 live sts rem on the side of the octagon, place these sts on the needle and continue with applied I-cord across. Pick up the 30 rem selvedge sts and continue working applied I-cord. BO, cut yarn, and knot to prevent fraying.

Pick up the 84 sts from the bottom of the panel and finish this edge with applied I-cord.

attach back to frame

Place the 72 live sts from the holder for the side of the rectangle onto a needle and hold these sts and needle parallel to the 72 sts picked up from the rectangle with needles facing the same way.

Fold the knitting over the frame to form a tube.

Use the three-needle bind-off (see "Special Knitting Techniques" appendix) to join the two sets of sts and attach the back to the frame.

Rep to attach the opposite side of the rectangle to the frame. It will be harder to work these sts because you will be stretching the back.

Fold tab over the top of the frame and attach with three-needle bind-off.

chair bottom

Holding two strands together, using straight or circular needles, CO 60 sts.

Begin working Linen Stitch with a slipped st selvedge as follows, slipping all stitches purlwise:

Row 1 (WS): Sl 1, (sl1 wyib, p1), end p1.

Row 2 (RS): Sl 1, (sl1 wyif, k1), end k1.

Rep these 2 rows until work measures 12½".

attach seat to frame

With RS facing, join new yarn and pick up and knit 56 sts using 1 leg of each selvedge st.

Row 1: Sl 1, (sl1 wyib, p1) 4 times, p38, (sl1 wyib, p1) 4 times, end p1.

Row 2: Sl 1, (sl1 wyif, k1) 4 times, k38, (sl1 wyif, k1) 4 times, end k1.

Rep these two rows until piece measures 5". Place sts on holder.

With WS facing, join new yarn and, on a new needle, pick up and knit 56 sts from other leg of selvedge st.

Rep for other side of seat.

Attach seat bottom to frame in the same manner you attached back to frame.

special knitting techniques

cast-ons

Backward Loop Cast-On

This cast-on is also called the *single cast-on* or the *backward-e cast-on.* You typically use this cast-on when you need to add stitches in the middle of a piece, and you will use just one needle.

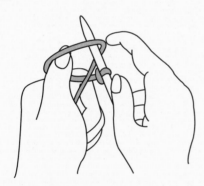

1. Make a slipknot and place it on the RH needle, or, if you are in the middle of a piece, turn the work, and hold the needle in your right hand.
2. Wrap the working yarn once around your left thumb with the yarn attached to the needle on the top and the yarn attached to the ball on the bottom.
3. Insert the needle into the thumb loop and slip it onto the needle.
4. Repeat steps 2 and 3 until you've cast on the appropriate number of stitches.

Knitted Cast-On

1. Make a slipknot and place it on the LH needle.
2. With the second needle, knit into this stitch, but do not slip the stitch off the needle. Instead, transfer this new stitch onto the LH needle.
3. Repeat step 2 until you have cast on the appropriate number of stitches.

Cable Cast-On

1. Make a slipknot and place it on the LH needle.
2. With the second needle, knit into this stitch, but do not slip the stitch off the needle. Instead, transfer this new stitch onto the LH needle.

3. Insert the RH needle between the last 2 stitches on the LH needle.

4. Wrap the yarn and pull the new stitch through, just as you do when knitting. Transfer the new stitch to the LH needle.

5. Repeat steps 3 and 4 until you have cast on the correct number of stitches.

Long-Tail Cast-On

Before you begin the long-tail cast-on, you need to estimate how long to make your tail. You can conservatively figure an inch per stitch, or approximately 4 times wider than whatever you are making (if your sweater is 20" across, you'll want a tail about 80" long). You will use only one needle. (Some knitters like to cast on around both needles held together and then pull one out at the end. This ensures that the cast-on edge is tidy, but not too tight.)

1. Make a slipknot and place it on the RH needle.

2. Hold the tail end with your left hand and the working yarn in your right hand.

3. Wrap the working yarn once around your left thumb.

4. Insert the needle into the thumb loop, but leave it on your thumb.

5. Wrap the yarn in your right hand around the needle.

6. Bring the needle through the loop on your thumb and move it toward you. Then gently snug up the stitch.

7. Repeat steps 3–6 until you've cast on the appropriate number of stitches.

Provisional Cast-On

1. Using a crochet hook and scrap yarn, crochet a chain several stitches longer than you need to cast on. Cut yarn and pull it through the last loop to secure it loosely. Mark this end by tying a knot in the tail. You will unravel the chain later from this end.

2. The back of each crochet chain has a bump in the center of the stitch. Insert the knitting needle through the third bump in the chain, wrap the working yarn around the needle, and draw the loop through. There is 1 st on the needle.

3. Insert the needle into the next bump on the chain, wrap the yarn around the needle and draw the loop through.

4. Repeat step 3 until you have the required number of stitches on the needle. Continue with the project until you are directed to return to the provisional cast-on.

5. Starting with the marked end, carefully unravel the crochet chain and transfer the live stitches to the needle as they are freed from the chain.

decreases

S2KP: (A centered double decrease.) Slip 2 stitches as if to k2tog. Knit 1 stitch. Pass the 2 slipped stitches over the stitch just knit.
SK2P: (A left-leaning double decrease.) Slip 1 stitch, k2tog, pass the slipped stitch over the stitch just made.
K3TOG: (A right-leaning double decrease.) Knit 3 stitches together as 1 stitch.

increases

KFB: (Knit in the front and the back of the next stitch.) Knit the next stitch normally, but do not slide it off the LH needle. Insert the RH needle into the back of the same stitch, behind the LH needle. Wrap the yarn and pull it through. Move both new stitches off the LH needle.
PFB: (Purl in the front and the back of the next stitch.) Purl the next stitch normally, but do not slide it off the LH needle. Insert the RH needle into the back of the same stitch by bringing it around in a U-turn and inserting the needle from

left to right. Purl this stitch and then move both new stitches off the LH needle.

M1: Make 1 increases are increases that are made between 2 stitches. There are two variations: one slants a bit to the left (M1L), the other a bit to the right (M1R). If a pattern does not specify M1L or M1R, choose whichever one you find easiest to work.

M1L (Make 1 Left): Lift the horizontal thread between stitches by inserting the left needle from front to back. Knit into the back of this stitch.

M1R (Make 1 Right): Lift the horizontal thread between stitches by inserting the left needle from back to front. Knit into the front of this stitch.

M1P (Make 1 Purl): Lift the horizontal thread between stitches by inserting the left needle from back to front. Purl into the front of this stitch.

Purl Double Increase: Purl into the front and back of the next stitch (see "pfb") and slide stitches from left needle. With the LH needle, pick up the purl bump from the stitch just worked and purl it through the back loop.

Yarn Overs

YO (before a knit stitch): Bring yarn to the front of the work, between the needles. Work the next stitch as specified, which will bring the yarn up over the needle creating an eyelet and an extra stitch.

YO (between purl stitches): The yarn is already in the front of the work. Bring yarn up over the needle, then down on the backside of the work and under the needle, back to the front, ready for the next purl stitch.

YO2: A double yarn over. Bring the yarn to the front between the needles. Wrap the yarn around the right needle once, bringing it back to the front of the work. Work the next stitch as specified. Individual patterns will describe whether you are to treat the double yarn over as 2 stitches or 1 stitch in the next row.

i-cord

I-cord is a skinny tube of knitting that is perfect for handles, straps, and ties. Use 2 double-pointed needles to make I-cord.

1. Cast on the specified number of stitches.
2. Knit the stitches on the needle, do not turn the work.
3. Slide the stitches to the other end of the needle, bringing the yarn snugly across the back of the work.
4. Repeat steps 2 and 3 until your I-cord is long enough.

picking up stitches

1. Working from right to left with the RS facing, insert the needle through the edge of the knitted work, working in the first row of complete stitches along the tops of pieces or in the ladder between stitches along the sides of pieces.

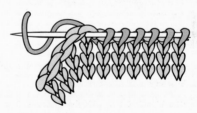

2. Wrap the needle as if to knit and pull the loop through to the RS.
3. Repeat steps 1 and 2, spacing your stitches evenly as described in the pattern.

kitchener stitch (grafting)

A method of joining two pieces almost invisibly by mimicking a row of knitting with a tapestry needle. With right sides facing you, place the pieces to be joined on a surface, each on its own needle, with the needles parallel to one another. Thread a tapestry needle with the working yarn.

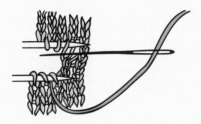

1. Insert the needle into the first stitch on the bottom needle as if to purl. Pull the yarn through. Leave the stitch on the needle.
2. Insert the needle into the first stitch on the top needle as if to knit. Pull the yarn through. Leave the stitch on the needle.
3. Insert the needle into the first stitch on the bottom needle again, but this time as if to knit. Slip the stitch off the knitting needle.
4. Insert the needle into the next stitch on the bottom needle as if to purl and leave it on the needle.
5. Insert the needle into the first stitch on the top needle again, this time as if to purl and slip it off the needle.
6. Insert the needle into the next stitch on the top needle, as if to knit. Leave this stitch on the needle.
7. Repeat steps 3–6 until all the stitches have been joined and slipped off the needle. *Remember, you will always go into a stitch twice.*

three-needle bind-off

The three-needle bind-off is used to join two pieces together without seaming. Put each set of stitches on a separate knitting needle. Hold the needles parallel in the left hand with right sides together and wrong sides facing out.

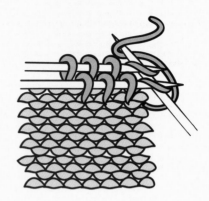

1. Insert a third needle (of the same size or slightly larger than the working needles) into the first stitch on the front needle and then the first stitch on the back needle. Knit these 2 stitches together.
2. Knit the next stitch on the front needle and the next stitch on the back needle together as in step 1.
3. Bring the outside stitch on the RH needle up over the inside stitch on the RH needle as you do to bind off.
4. Repeat steps 2 and 3 until all the stitches are bound off. Cut yarn and pull through the last loop to secure.

wrap & turn

To add partial rows (or *short rows*) to create shaping, you have to turn around in the middle of a row. To do so without creating a hole, you must "wrap" the turning stitches as follows:

1. Work to the specified stitch in the pattern. Slip the next stitch to the RH needle.
2. Bring yarn to the opposite side of the work.
3. Slip the stitch back to the LH needle.
4. Turn your work and bring the yarn to the correct position to work this next row.
5. Repeat these 4 steps as described in the pattern.

When you encounter a wrapped stitch in subsequent rows:

1. Slip the wrapped stitch onto the RH needle.
2. Insert the LH needle into the wrap at the base of the stitch from bottom to top.
3. Slip the wrapped stitch back to the LH needle.
4. Knit (or purl) the wrap and the stitch together.

crochet techniques
Chain Stitch (Ch)

1. Make a slipknot for the first stitch if you do not already have a stitch on the hook.
2. Wrap the yarn around the hook from back to front and catch it with the end of the hook.
3. Bring this loop through the stitch on the hook. There is 1 loop on the hook.
4. Repeat steps 2 and 3 for each chain stitch required.

Single Crochet (SC)

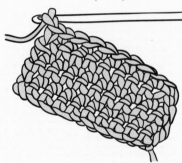

You will have 1 loop on the hook to begin.

1. Insert the hook into the work as the pattern directs.
2. Wrap the yarn around the hook and pull it through the work. There are 2 loops on the hook.
3. Wrap the yarn and pull it through 2 loops. There is 1 loop on the hook.
4. Repeat steps 1–3 for each single crochet.

Double Crochet (DC)

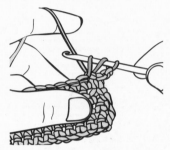

You will have 1 loop on the hook to begin.

1. Wrap the yarn around the hook.
2. Insert the hook into the work as the pattern directs.
3. Wrap the yarn around the hook and pull it through the work. There are 3 loops on the hook.
4. Wrap the yarn around the hook and pull it through 2 loops. There are 2 loops on the hook.
5. Wrap the yarn around the hook and pull it through 2 loops. There is 1 loop on the hook.
6. Repeat steps 1–5 for each double crochet.

knitting
abbreviations

Abbreviation	Meaning
alt	alternate
beg	begin(ning)
BO	bind off (cast off)
CC	contrasting color
CN	cable needle
CO	cast on
cont	continue(ing)
dc	double crochet
dec	decrease(ing)
dpn(s)	double-pointed needle(s)
foll	follow(s)(ing)
g	grams
inc	increase(ing)
k	knit
k tbl	knit through back of loop
k2tog	knit 2 sts together (right-leaning decrease)
k2tog tbl	knit 2 sts together through the back loops (left-leaning decrease)
k3tog	knit 3 sts together (right-leaning double decrease)
k3tog tbl	knit 3 sts together through the back loops (left-leaning double decrease)
kfb	knit into front and back of stitch (increase)
LH	left hand
m	meter(s)
M1	make 1 (increase between stitches)
M1L	make 1 left
M1R	make 1 right
M1P	make 1 purl
MC	main color
mm	millimeters
oz	ounce(s)
p	purl
p2tog	purl 2 sts together (decrease)
p2tog-tbl	purl 2 sts together through back loop (decrease)
patt(s)	pattern(s)

Abbreviation	Meaning
pfb	purl into front and back of stitch (increase)
pm	place marker
psso	pass slipped stitch(es) over
rem	remaining
rep	repeat
rev St st	reverse stockinette stitch
RH	right hand
rib	ribbing
RS	right side(s)
s2kp	slip 2 sts as if to k2tog, k1, pass the slipped sts over
sc	single crochet
sk2p	slip 1 st, k2tog, pass slipped st over
skp	slip 1 st as if to knit, k1, pass the slipped st over
sl	slip (slip sts purlwise, unless directed otherwise)
sl st	slip stitch
sm	slip marker
ssk	slip 2 sts as if to knit, one at a time, then k those 2 sts together
ssp	slip 2 sts as if to purl, one at a time, then p those 2 sts together
st(s)	stitch(es)
St st	stockinette stitch
tbl	through back of loop(s)
tog	together
w&t	wrap and turn
WS	wrong side(s)
wyib	with yarn in back
wyif	with yarn in front
yd.	yard(s)
YO	yarn over
YO2	yarn over twice
* *	repeat directions between *s as indicated
[]	repeat directions within brackets as many times as indicated

Learn more about the highlighted terms in the "Special Knitting Techniques" appendix.

contributing designers

Eileen Adler

As a little girl, Eileen Adler dreamed about the day when she would become a member of "the knitting group," but first she had to learn to knit! On a summer afternoon, her mother demonstrated a few stitches, watched the laborious execution of a few, and with her encouragement, Eileen learned to knit. Over time, Eileen has carefully orchestrated a knitting life that encompasses designing, teaching, and writing. Knitting is her constant companion because within her hands she holds her heart—the unequivocal gratitude for her mother's patience and insight, and for so many others who continue to enrich her journey every day.

Sarah Barbour

After several false starts as a child, Sarah Barbour finally learned to knit nine years ago and now she can't stop. She teaches both knitting and crochet, and has been designing professionally for three years. She decided early on that knitting should be for all seasons, so she is excited to contribute a design to this book. Sarah lives in central Illinois with her husband and two daughters, the older of whom has just learned to crochet. She is expecting her third daughter around the same time this book hits the shelves. You can find her online at www.ropeknits.com.

Heather Broadhurst

Heather Broadhurst, known as the Walkabout Knitter and self-proclaimed queen of short rows, has a well-deserved reputation for knitting almost anything with almost anything. When she's not writing about the wonders of relational databases, working on her MLIS, or playing Linux network geek, Heather is often found knitting while she's out walking around San Diego, California, where she also teaches new knitters in bars, coffeehouses, and hospitals.

Rachel "Ivy" Clarke

Rachel "Ivy" Clarke is a librarian at the Fashion Institute of Design and Merchandising in Los Angeles, California, which exposes her to two of her favorite things: knitwear design and warm weather. She is a regular contributor to www.metapostmodernknitting.com.

Carol Feller

Carol Feller is an independent knitwear designer living in Cork, Ireland. Trained as both an artist and a structural engineer, she has found a real "home" in knitting and design, which allows her to combine the best of both worlds. As a busy mother of four, finding time to design is not always easy, but she does her best. Carol's patterns have been published in *Knitty* (www.knitty.com) and the *Twist Collective* (www.twistcollective.com). More patterns are available from her personal Web site at www.stolenstitches.com. Living in Ireland, Carol rarely gets a chance to knit for warm weather, although she often dreams of a climate where you can wear a light bamboo top every day!

Faina Goberstein

Faina Goberstein grew up in Russia, where knowing how to knit is a necessity. Although Faina chose a different profession in life, she completed a two-year course on knitting design. While working as a design engineer in Russia, she continued to create and design knitwear. After she immigrated to the United States, Faina changed her career path and began teaching mathematics at a community college. She sees an unquestionable connection between mathematics, knitting, and engineering design. Faina co-authored *Casual, Elegant Knits* in 2008. Her designs have also appeared in *Interweave Knits* and *Knitscene*. She lives in Chico, California, where designing for a warm climate comes naturally.

Stefanie Japel

Stefanie Japel is the author of *Glam Knits* and the popular *Fitted Knits*. Her designs are featured on all popular knitting Web sites, such as *Knitty*, and magazines, such as *Knitscene* and *Interweave Knits,* as well as in books, including *Stitch 'n' Bitch Nation, Knit Wit, Not Another Teen Knitting Book, KnitGrrl,* and *Big Girl Knits.* Her Web site, www.glampyre.com, is where Stefanie posts her blog, sells original pattern designs, and offers free patterns. She lives in New Mexico with her husband and baby daughter.

Janine Le Cras

Janine Le Cras lives, works, knits, and windsurfs on the tiny island of Guernsey in the middle of the English Channel. Her affinity to sea and sand made designing for this book a match made in heaven. The mother of two grown children, she divides her time between her computer, knitting needles, spinning wheel, and the beach. Janine has designed for several online magazines such as *MagKnits, The Inside Loop*, and *Knotions*. She also works closely with the Unique Sheep (http://uniquesheep.com) on designs that showcase their wonderful yarns. You can visit her blog at guernseygal.typepad.com/knitting_on_an_island/, or find her on Ravelry as Guernseygal.

Dawn Leeseman

Dawn Leeseman has been knitting for over 25 years and working as a freelance designer for the past 5 years. She currently designs, edits, and rewrites Japanese patterns for Crystal Palace Yarns. Dawn's designs have been published by Y2Knit patterns, and in *Vogue Knitting, Interweave Knits, Knit 'N Style, One-Skein Wonders,* and *Pampered Pooches.* Dawn is also the coauthor of *Casual, Elegant Knit*s. When she is not designing and knitting, she teaches knitting classes at HeartStrings Yarn Studio in Chico, California, where she also resides.

Lisa Limber

Lisa Limber began knitting 35 years ago and has not stopped since. After many years in the corporate world, she now makes her living as a knitwear designer, a yarn rep, and teaching knitting workshops throughout southern California. Her design inspirations come from the time she spends working with yarn stores, where she sees new ideas every day, and through her local knitting guild, where she shares ideas with other knitters. When she is not on the road working with her customers, she spends her knitting time with her best friend, Zoe, her Cairn Terrier.

Anne Kuo Lukito

If it weren't for bouts of insomnia, Anne Kuo Lukito would never find time to knit or use up her abundance of creative energy. Or is it the other way around? Anne is co-owner of Handicraft Cafe (www.handicraftcafe.com) and talks about her crafty endeavors on her blog, http://craftdiversions.wordpress.com. Anne's designs have been published in *Knitty, Luxury One-Skein Wonders,* and *Interweave Knits.*

Marnie MacLean

Marnie MacLean has been knitting for most of her life, but didn't take up designing until she moved to Los Angeles, California, where she quickly learned the challenges of designing for a warm climate. Now that she's living in Portland, Oregon, Marnie's thankful for all the excuses to don her warm woolens, but she still finds plenty of opportunities to show off her lighter pieces as well. You can see all of her designs and tutorials on her blog at http://marniemaclean.com.

Jairlyn Mason

Jairlyn Mason grew up in the Los Angeles area and has been active in the fiber arts her entire life. She knits, crochets, sews, weaves, dyes fabrics, designs costumes, and has a particular weakness for knitted toys. She attained a BFA in 3D Media: Fiber from Cal State Long Beach. You can find her designs online at www.knitty.com and www.tillitomas.com. She also writes custom patterns for Compatto Yarn Salon in Santa Monica, California, and is a staff costume designer for the Center Theatre Group's "Ready, Set, P.L.A.Y." children's theatre program. She hopes to continue working as a costume designer in educational children's theatre.

Jillian Moreno

Jillian Moreno is the co-author of *Big Girl Knits* and *More Big Girls Knits,* and her work is featured in more than a dozen books. Jillian designs the *Curvy Knits* series for Classic Elite Yarns and is the editor of *Knittyspin.com.* She is still amazed that she gets to play with fiber for a job. Jillian lives in Ann Arbor, Michigan, with her husband, two kids, and a lot of yarn.

Kendra Nitta

Kendra Nitta has lived most of her life in sunny California. She spends her free time knitting, sewing, designing, and writing about all of it at http://missknitta.com. Her work has also appeared in *Knitty* and *Luxury Yarn One-Skein Wonders.*

Amy Polcyn

Amy Polcyn is a knitwear designer and technical editor living in suburban Detroit, Michigan, with her husband, daughter, and two wool-loving cats. Previously an elementary school teacher, she turned to a full-time life in the fiber world in 2007. Amy's work has been featured in most major knitting magazines, numerous yarn company collections, and several books, and she is perhaps best known for her knitted sushi pattern originally featured in *MagKnits.* Her favorite techniques are cables and textured patterns, with the occasional dash of colorwork thrown in. Warm weather is her favorite time to knit, as there's nothing like relaxing on a sunny beach or in the park with a project. In her spare time, Amy enjoys tap and belly dancing, spinning yarn, and reading. She blogs about all things knitting at http://frottez.blogspot.com.

Susan Robicheau

Susan Robicheau has been a freelance designer for several years and lives in Nova Scotia, Canada, where the temperatures can soar during the summer months. At age six, Susan began learning how to design and knit clothes for her dolls. Knitting has taught her so many skills that help in life, such as patience, eye-hand coordination, attention to detail, time management, and working as part of a team. There are always new yarns, knitting needles, and tools to try. Watching fashion and color trends and translating those into new designs is always exciting. Two simple stitches provide endless possibilities and challenges.

Sarah Sutherland

Sarah Sutherland knits in the Canadian Prairies. She knows that a passion for the needles cannot be put down just because the weather gets warm and that it would be horrible to have to give it up just because one happens to live in balmy climes, so warm-weather patterns are a necessity. After a few false starts over the years, she has been knitting diligently in all seasons since 2002 and has been designing since 2005. She has published cool-weather patterns in *Knitty* and *MagKnits*. She blogs at http://parallaxknitting.com.

Julia Trice

Julia Trice is an attorney and an avid knitter who dabbles in knit design in her spare time. She has published designs in two books, *Greetings from Knit Cafe* and *Boho Baby,* and in *Knitty,* an online magazine. She lives in southern California with her husband and her adorable newborn son.

Katherine Vaughan

Katherine Vaughan is an academic librarian by day, knitter and designer of warm-weather garments and accessories by night. Her favorite creations are decorative, wool-free items for women and children. She watches movies in sunny North Carolina with her husband, preschooler, and a succession of short-lived goldfish.

Tonya Wagner

Tonya Wagner taught herself to knit when she should have been studying for finals. She started frequenting her local yarn store, the Knit Nook, to satisfy her fiber addiction and soon began working and teaching classes there. Tonya considers herself lucky that her husband is a professional musician; there's no better time to knit in public than while listening to live music. These days, Tonya usually knits at home while taking care of her toddler, Leo. You can find Tonya's patterns, tutorials, and more on her blog at www.theshizknit.com.

yarn sources

The following companies have generously provided the yarns used for the projects in *Knitting in the Sun*. Find out more about the companies and where you can find their products through the Web sites listed below, or visit your local yarn shop for help selecting yarns.

Berroco
www.berroco.com

Cascade Yarns
www.cascadeyarns.com

Classic Elite
www.classiceliteyarns.com

Coats Crochet
www.coatsandclark.com

Curious Creek Fibers
www.curiouscreek.com

Dream in Color
www.dreamincoloryarn.com

K1C2
www.k1c2.com

Lanaknits Hemp for Knitting
www.lanaknits.com

Lorna's Laces
www.lornaslaces.net

Louet
www.louet.com

Malabrigo
www.malabrigoyarn.com

Nashua Handknits
www.nashuaknits.com

Rowan
www.knitrowan.com

South West Trading Company (SWTC)
www.soysilk.com

Trendsetter
www.trendsetteryarns.com

index

about the author

Kristi Porter is an author, designer, technical editor, and teacher. In addition to authoring *Knitting for Dogs* (Simon & Schuster, 2005) and *Knitting Patterns For Dummies* (Wiley Publishing, Inc., 2007), her work has been featured in the *Knitgrrl* series, the *Big Girl Knits* series, *No Sheep for You*, and *KnitWit*. She is a frequent contributor to *Knitty* and has been a part of the online magazine since its start in 2002.

Kristi doesn't remember learning to knit as a child, but she captured the basics and an enthusiasm for the craft from her mother, her aunt, and her grandmother. She began her first projects as a designer and a knitter, realizing only later that not everyone designed their own patterns. Although her first attempts were boxy and oversized, once she grasped the importance of gauge, she was on her way to creating wearable designs.

As a knitter and teacher in Southern California, Kristi knows well what warm-weather knitters want. Choosing projects and guiding her students in creating garments that they will enjoy knitting—and enjoy wearing—has helped her understand the need for designs specifically created for warmer climates.

Kristi designs and teaches in sunny La Jolla, California, where she makes her home with her husband and two daughters.